Top Dogs and Fat Cats

TOP DOGS AND FAT CATS

The Debate on High Pay

EDITED BY J. R. SHACKLETON

with contributions from

ALEX EDMANS • LUKE HILDYARD • SOPHIE JARVIS
DAMIEN KNIGHT • REBECCA LOWE • HARRY MCCREDDIE
PAUL ORMEROD • VICKY PRYCE • J. R. SHACKLETON
JUDY Z. STEPHENSON • ALEX WILD

Institute of
Economic Affairs

First published in Great Britain in 2019 by
The Institute of Economic Affairs
2 Lord North Street
Westminster
London SW1P 3LB
in association with London Publishing Partnership Ltd
www.londonpublishingpartnership.co.uk

The mission of the Institute of Economic Affairs is to improve understanding
of the fundamental institutions of a free society by analysing and expounding
the role of markets in solving economic and social problems.

A CIP catalogue record for this book is available from the British Library.

ISBN 978-0-255-36773-8

Many IEA publications are translated into languages other
than English or are reprinted. Permission to translate or to reprint
should be sought from the Director General at the address above.

Typeset in Kepler by T&T Productions Ltd
www.tandtproductions.com

Printed and bound in Great Britain by Hobbs the Printers Ltd

CONTENTS

Alex Edmans

Alex Edmans is Professor of Finance at London Business School. He has spoken at the World Economic Forum in Davos, testified in the UK Parliament, given a TED talk on 'What to Trust in a Post-Truth World' and a TEDx talk on 'The Social Responsibility of Business'. He is also Mercers' School Memorial Professor of Business at Gresham College and Managing Editor of the *Review of Finance*, the leading academic finance journal in Europe. Alex has a BA from the University of Oxford and a PhD from MIT and was previously a tenured professor at Wharton, where he won fourteen teaching awards in six years.

Luke Hildyard

Luke Hildyard is Director of the High Pay Centre think-tank, where he previously worked as Deputy Director from 2012 to 2015. He was subsequently Policy Lead for Corporate Governance and Stewardship at the Pensions and Lifetime Savings Association, the trade body for UK pension fund investors, before returning to HPC in March 2018. He has authored reports on subjects including pay, corporate governance and responsible investment and has also previously worked for a number of think-tanks and in local government.

Sophie Jarvis

After graduating from the University of Bristol with a degree in classics and a short stint in the insurance market, Sophie Jarvis joined the Adam Smith Institute in 2017. She is now the Head of Government Affairs for the ASI and a regular political commentator in the national media. Her areas of research include the gender pay gap, childcare regulation, the rail industry and entrepreneurship.

Damien Knight

Damien Knight is an executive remuneration consultant with over 40 years' experience. He is currently working with MM&K, the independent remuneration consultancy based in the City of London, and was previously with Hay Group, Aon Consulting and Watson Wyatt. He has advised the remuneration committees and management of several FTSE-100 companies and other international groups. At MM&K he has worked closely with Minerva, the proxy agency, influencing government policy on remuneration governance and disclosure legislation, and producing authoritative research on historical pay and company performance in listed companies. Damien has a physics degree from the University of Oxford. He was co-editor of the *Executive Compensation Handbook* (Free Press).

Rebecca Lowe

Rebecca Lowe is the Director of FREER, a new initiative promoting economically and socially liberal thinking. She is also a Research Fellow at the Institute of Economic Affairs. She has worked for various political research organisations, as a political consultant, and in the arts and education sectors. She was State and Society Fellow, and Convenor of the Research Group on Political Thought, at Policy Exchange. Her interests lie within political philosophy and economics. Rebecca is undertaking part-time doctoral research at King's College London, in the Department of Political Economy.

Harry McCreddie

Harry McCreddie is a research analyst at the remuneration consultancy MM&K. He studied at the University of Exeter, where he received a first-class degree in mathematics. As well as carrying out extensive remuneration benchmarking work and associated business analysis, he is expert in building models for share plan valuation (and IFRS2 accounting charges).

Paul Ormerod

Currently a visiting professor in computer science at University College London, Paul Ormerod is an economist, author and entrepreneur. Paul read economics at the University of Cambridge and took an MPhil in economics at the University of Oxford. He is a Fellow of the British Academy of Social Sciences, and in 2009 was awarded a DSc *honoris causa* by the University of Durham for the distinction of his contribution to economics. Paul has published four best-selling books on economics: *Death of Economics*, *Butterfly Economics*, *Why Most Things Fail* and *Positive Linking*. In 2018 a volume of his weekly *City AM* articles was published by the IEA as *Against the Grain: Insights from an Economic Contrarian*. He was a founder of the Henley Centre for Forecasting Ltd., which the management sold to WPP Group in the 1990s.

Vicky Pryce

Vicky Pryce is Chief Economic Adviser at the Centre for Economics and Business Research. She was previously Senior Managing Director at FTI Consulting, DG for Economics at BIS and Joint Head of the UK Government Economic Service. Before that she was Partner at KPMG after senior economic positions in banking and the oil sector. She holds a number of academic posts and is author or co-author of numerous books. She is a Fellow and Council member of the UK Academy for Social Sciences, a Fellow of the Society of Professional Economists and a Companion of the British Academy of Management. She sits on the Council of the Institute for Fiscal Studies and on the Economic Advisory Group of the British Chambers of Commerce.

J. R. Shackleton

Len Shackleton is Professor of Economics at the University of Buckingham, a Research and Editorial Fellow at the IEA and Editor of *Economic Affairs*. He has run two major business schools and worked as an economist in the UK civil service. His main research interests are in labour economics.

Judy Z. Stephenson

Judy Stephenson worked in advertising and communication before obtaining her PhD in the Department of Economic History at the LSE. She is currently the David Richards Junior Research Fellow at Wadham College, Oxford, and a Research Associate at UCL's Bartlett School of Construction and Project Management.

Alex Wild

Alex Wild is a Director at Public First, a research and campaign consultancy. Alex spent five years at the TaxPayers' Alliance (TPA), for most of that time as Research Director. He was responsible for the research output of the TPA and has frequently appeared on national broadcast media. Previously Alex worked as a researcher on Boris Johnson's successful 2012 London Mayoral campaign and as an analyst at an economic, business and market research firm in Delhi.

SUMMARY

- In contrast to the recent past when even Labour politicians were 'intensely relaxed' about high pay, there is now widespread concern about the apparent excesses of some pay structures in corporate businesses.
- Top pay has risen much faster than average levels of pay in the last twenty years. This is in part the consequence of globalisation and developments in communications technology, but it may also be a result of rigged markets and 'crony capitalism'.
- It is asserted that shareholders do not have enough influence on setting executive pay, which is determined by remuneration committees and consultants with a vested interest in boosting top pay.
- The public seems to distinguish between remuneration for CEOs – who are essentially employees of large businesses – and that of entrepreneurs, entertainers and sports stars, whose earnings and wealth can more easily be understood as related to their abilities and efforts.
- It is important to understand how pay data are produced and used. It is also important when assessing sensitivity to performance to look at changes

in wealth (as a result of changes in share prices) rather than simply at the current pay package.

- In looking at trends over time we need to distinguish between pay *awarded* and pay *realised*. It may be that political pressures have recently reduced the reward for future performance, but this will not be reflected for a while in currently realised pay, the basis for which will have been set some time previously.
- A claim is often made that CEO pay bears no relationship to company performance. To assess this claim requires rather more sophisticated analysis than is often employed by activists and the media. Using such analysis it does seem that pay reacts (both positively and negatively) to changes in performance, though possibly less than it should.
- The widespread adoption of Long-Term Incentive Plans (LTIPs) has been widely criticised; it is felt that these schemes are often badly designed and have led to unnecessary inflation of executive pay.
- Politicians and electors are also concerned about high pay in the public sector, and in sectors where government funding plays a major role, such as universities, academy schools and many charities. This has led to informal pay caps being administered by regulators.
- There is a 'gender dimension' to high pay: women are underrepresented among very high earners. This does not appear, however, to be the consequence of discrimination, but rather the result of choices and lifestyles which differ between men and women.

This may be in part the consequence of inadequate information and networks.

- Governments need to be careful in how they react to populist calls for action. The current requirement for large businesses to spell out the basis of their pay structure may be acceptable, and maintaining a watchful eye on pay in the public sector is sensible. But giving the state power permanently to fix pay ratios or even pay caps brings dangers which are not sufficiently discussed by those demanding government intervention.

TABLES AND FIGURES

1   INTRODUCTION

J. R. Shackleton

Background

Politicians are more concerned with other people's pay than ever before. Some of this concern is of long standing, though today's policies are taking a different form from those in the past. In recent years, for example, we have developed a complex system of ever-increasing minimum wages. We require large organisations to publish their gender pay gaps (soon, probably, their ethnic pay gaps as well) and work towards narrowing them.

Such concerns are understandable, and policies are aimed at improving the circumstances of definable groups of disadvantaged people – low-paid workers, underpaid women and so forth. Classical liberals might nevertheless question the principle behind these interventions. Richard Epstein (1992: 149), for example, asserts that

> the terms of an employment contract are the business of only the parties to it. Freedom of contract on this matter is no different from freedom of speech or freedom of action ... unless the contract in question poses the threat of harm to third parties or is procured by fraud or sharp practice.

Other critics might argue about the form which policies take, or worry about their effectiveness, or their knock-on consequences – which may in some cases damage the very groups that are intended to benefit. But the purpose of such interventions fits into a long tradition of policy concern for redistribution and assistance to the less-well-off. However, the issues covered in this book do not concern policies aimed in any very clear way at improving the position of disadvantaged groups.

Large amounts of information of varying accuracy are being published about the pay of FTSE-100 chief executives, footballers, movie stars and other people in the public eye such as newsreaders, university vice-chancellors and heads of large charities. Here political interventions – actual and proposed – and social media pressure (which is often as powerful as deliberate government intervention) are not aimed at improving the circumstances of any individuals at all. Rather, politicians and activists are attacking the moral basis of what they regard as over-generous rewards thrown up by the market economy, and demanding their suppression.

This concern for social justice, admirable as it may seem, presents problems. For, as Hayek (1976: 58) wrote:

> No agreement exists about what social justice requires ... no preconceived scheme of distribution could be effectively devised in a society whose individuals are free ... though a great many people are dissatisfied with the existing pattern of distribution, none of them has really any clear idea of what pattern he would regard as 'just'.

This is certainly true. Even among those opposed to high pay, concern is oddly selective. While listed company executives are commonly excoriated, entrepreneurs often get a free pass. Some people are quite happy with footballers being paid enormous amounts for kicking a ball around, but get cross about radio DJs being paid a packet.

Be that as it may, in just a few years views seem to have shifted sharply to become much more critical of all high earners. We have moved from a cross-party neutrality about the acceptability of high pay – most famously encapsulated by Labour minister Peter Mandelson being 'intensely relaxed about people getting filthy rich'[1] – to Conservative minister Caroline Nokes asserting that no one should get a salary of more than £1 million a year.[2]

Theresa May promised to attack high executive pay when she became Prime Minister, returning intermittently to this theme. One result is that regulation now requires UK quoted companies with more than 250 employees to publish the pay ratio between their CEO and average employee and justify its size. Companies must also publish a narrative explaining changes to the pay ratio from year to year and set them into the context of pay across the workforce.

The government has also started to use regulators to attack high pay in quasi-public sector areas such as universities

---

1 To be fair, Mandelson added the rider 'so long as they pay their taxes'.

2 No one should get a £1m salary, says Tory minister Caroline Nokes, *The Times*, 22 November 2018 (https://www.thetimes.co.uk/article/no-one-should-get-a-1m-salary-says-tory-minister-caroline-nokes-llq9sjnxx).

and academy school trusts, with institutions being required to justify any executive salaries over £150,000.[3]

Opposition leader Jeremy Corbyn and Shadow Chancellor John McDonnell have at various times threatened to give workers a direct say in executive pay in large companies through requiring worker representation on boards, and to impose pay caps (maximum ratios of top pay to that of the lowest paid) on the public sector, on utilities they hope to renationalise and on firms working on government contracts.

Research for *The Independent* in January 2017[4] suggested that Mr Corbyn's proposed pay caps were supported by 57 per cent of the public. Just 30 per cent of those surveyed disagreed with the idea that the government should set a limit, while 13 per cent said 'don't know'. Even among Conservative voters, 47 per cent agreed with Mr Corbyn, with only 40 per cent being opposed.

More moderate Labour MPs also want to see government action to constrain high pay. Rachel Reeves, Chair

---

3   See: Letter to academy trusts about levels of executive pay, Education and Skills Funding Agency, 4 December 2017 (https://assets.publishing. service.gov.uk/government/uploads/system/uploads/attachment_data/ file/665813/Letter_to_academy_trusts_about_levels_of_executive_pay .pdf). And: Vice-chancellors must justify their salaries, which will be published annually, Office for Students, 19 June 2018 (https://www .officeforstudents.org.uk/news-blog-and-events/press-and-media/ vice-chancellors-must-justify-their-salaries-which-will-be-published -annually/).

4   Majority of public support Jeremy Corbyn's plans to cap bosses' salaries, poll suggests, *The Independent*, 14 January 2017 (https://www.independent .co.uk/news/uk/politics/majority-of-public-support-jeremy-corbyn-s -plans-to-cap-bosses-salaries-poll-finds-a7527381.html).

of the Commons business committee and an ex-Bank of England economist, has said that government should take tougher measures on pay if company boards, and the remuneration committees that set executive pay, fail to exercise moderation.[5] She has argued that 'excessive executive pay undermines public trust in business. When CEOs are happily banking ever-larger bonuses while average worker pay is squeezed, then something is going very wrong.' And fear that public trust in their particular housebuilding business was being undermined by the huge bonuses paid to their CEO, Jeff Fairburn, led the Persimmon board to sack him in November 2018.[6]

So top pay is clearly a very important issue, and is explored in contrasting ways by the contributors to this book.

Executive pay

Luke Hildyard of the High Pay Centre begins the discussion by setting out the indictment against excessive CEO pay. He points out that executive remuneration in the UK has risen far faster than that of ordinary workers in recent decades, and claims that this has occurred without any corresponding improvement in company performance.

---

5   Top pay in UK up by 11% as workers' wages fail to match inflation, *The Guardian*, 15 August 2018 (https://www.theguardian.com/business/2018/aug/15/uk-top-bosses-pay-rise-average-earnings-hit-39m-2017-high-pay-centre).

6   Persimmon boss asked to leave amid outrage over bonus, *The Guardian*, 7 November 2018 (https://www.theguardian.com/business/2018/nov/07/persimmon-boss-asked-to-leave-amid-ongoing-outrage-over-bonus).

He dismisses the idea that international competition for rare talent justifies high CEO pay, pointing out that most firms promote their CEOs from within the company. His analysis suggests that long-established successful businesses (as opposed to entrepreneurial start-ups) are built on effective organisational systems rather than the abilities of the current incumbent CEO, who therefore has in many cases rather little influence over a company's success. He draws attention, too, to elements of 'crony capitalism' that give many big businesses protected markets through their strong links to government.

Hildyard suggests that the ultimate providers of capital – the beneficial owners of company shares – would like to see more modest levels of executive pay, but they are separated from the operation of corporations by a web of financial advisors, asset managers and pension funds. These intermediaries are themselves highly paid and see no problem in paying company executives generously.

Listed companies are required to have remuneration committees which are independent of the company's management structure, but members of these committees are themselves well-remunerated, are from similar backgrounds to company executives and often hold, or have held, executive posts at other companies. The committees are advised by consultants who devise complex remuneration schemes to justify their existence, and act to bid up pay.

In Hildyard's view, this unsatisfactory situation is undermining the case for capitalism. Free-marketeers should be worried about this, and support reforms including worker representation on boards and remuneration committees, more detailed disclosure of pay structures and a requirement for institutional investors to consult ultimate beneficiaries on pay issues.

In their chapter, Damien Knight and Harry McCreddie offer a critical take on the way in which top pay data are presented and interpreted. They argue that 'journalists and consequently politicians have been persuaded by research and analysis which is fundamentally flawed'.

In their view CEO pay is not by any means out of control. Given that most schemes involve pay linked to future performance in various ways – often with long time lags – pay awards *granted* and pay awards *realised* in a period can be very different. In reporting, these measures are often confused, in some cases deliberately. Knight and McCreddie argue that, although pay awards achieved have been rising recently, pay granted has fallen, which means that pay received will fall in coming years.

They also demonstrate that journalists and others frequently err because they do not understand how to interpret data – most obviously in frequent claims that there is no relation between pay and performance.

Their view is that poor analysis has done more damage to the reputation of business – and to social cohesion – than companies have done by their executive pay policies. It has created a bandwagon on which too many ostensible supporters of business have felt obliged to climb.

Alex Edmans also criticises much writing on executive pay. Drawing on his own and others' academic research, he demolishes a number of myths associated with the case against CEO pay. For example, he shows that, contrary to popular belief, CEOs who perform badly do suffer financially – though he points out that it is their *wealth* rather than their income which is affected, as much of their remuneration is in company shares and share options which lose value with poor performance.

While Edmans believes strongly in the reform of company pay, he argues that disclosure of CEO/average pay ratios (a feature of Theresa May's policy) can lead to inappropriate conclusions and have unintended consequences which may harm workers. For example, firms may outsource low-paid work to improve their showing.

Edmans argues that reform efforts should focus on the *structure* of pay schemes, rather than the *level* of chief executive pay. Current pay schemes are complex, opaque and encourage short-termism. In particular, he argues that the use of LTIPs (Long-Term Incentive Plans) allows for 'gaming and fudging'. He advocates instead that pay should simply be in cash and shares with a long holding period. If shares can at the same time be awarded to employees, they will gain in line with CEOs, which will help address concerns about fairness.

In her chapter, Vicky Pryce examines high executive pay in an international context. She points out that the phenomenon of rising pay for top executives is found in many countries, not just in the US and the UK. In continental Europe she highlights Germany. Large German companies are often held up as a good example of corporate governance, with wider stakeholder interests, including employees, represented on supervisory boards. Many British commentators argue that such representation will tend to inhibit excessive pay awards. However, as Pryce points out, CEOs of some leading German firms are paid extremely generously. She puts this down to the need to compete for international talent.

Pryce also notes that, while the make-up of remuneration (the mix of salary, bonuses, shares and share options and so on) seems to differ in different parts of the world, high executive pay is also becoming a feature in Asia and Africa. She further points out that in some countries, for example China, recorded pay may understate the advantage executives enjoy from employment, as they also have access to a range of other benefits.

Pryce notes that there is considerable opposition to excessive executive pay in many countries, although opinion polls suggest that antipathy is, perhaps oddly, rather less marked in those countries where executive pay is highest. Governments have been inhibited in their responses, she suggests, because they are concerned that precipitate action might produce little gain. International cooperation might encourage them to overcome their scruples, but so far this has been limited to some minor European Union initiatives.

In his chapter, Paul Ormerod tackles the differing reasons for the high pay received by entrepreneurs, top sports and entertainment stars (which is in his view acceptable) and by executives of large corporations (which isn't).

Entrepreneurs provide a product or service which did not previously exist, and are thus able to secure monopoly profits, at least until competitors produce something equivalent or superior. These high returns (whether in salaries or in personal wealth through share ownership) are a necessary stimulant to invention and innovation.

Top athletes, artists and performers possess unusual talents which have been increasingly rewarded in recent decades as advances in communications technology have created worldwide markets for their services. But their highly visible achievements typically require exceptional personal effort and are not subject to great popular resentment.

By contrast, Ormerod argues, executive pay has risen for reasons which have little to do with improved performance and exceptional individual effort. Drawing on network analysis, he argues that board opinions in favour of high pay have spread for reasons which defy traditional notions of rational, optimal behaviour. Networks of non-executive directors, management consultants and remuneration experts have in effect facilitated successful rent-seeking by CEOs.

Other concerns

Judy Stephenson and Sophie Jarvis discuss the position of women in the top pay debate. While they recognise that women appear to be under-represented among top earners, they resist simplistic explanations in terms of discrimination and victimhood. They point out that the gender pay gap is widely misunderstood to involve women being paid less than men for the same work, when it is rather that men and women do different jobs, or work different hours, or have less continuous work experience. While this is partly the result of different choices and preferences, these are themselves gendered and reflect social, family and cultural expectations which are difficult to change.

In an illuminating analysis, Stephenson and Jarvis see the labour market as essentially an 'information market' concerning job opportunities and workplace behaviours. Improving the flow of information to women is an essential element in improving employment trajectories and the possibility of higher pay. This may also be an analysis which has relevance to ethnic pay gaps: many ethnic groups are similarly under-represented in high-paying jobs.

Stephenson and Jarvis welcome publication of gender pay gap data as a step towards improved information flows, while cautioning against 'positive discrimination' policies such as board quotas. The end goal should always be equality of opportunity rather than forced equality of outcome.

Alex Wild shifts the discussion to the public sector, where the arguments for limiting high pay are apparently clearer. Wild points out that, particularly taking pensions and other benefits into account, lower-paid workers do markedly better in the public sector than in the private sector. But top earners in the public sector are paid substantially less than top earners in the private sector.

However, few public sector jobs are directly comparable to those in the private sector. There are very limited opportunities in the public sector for independent judgement and actions, as politicians inevitably determine broad policy. There is also much less risk for people working in the public sector, as in most cases predetermined revenue comes from the government rather than the consumer. Senior civil servants, local authority chief executives and similar functionaries face many problems, but they do not operate in the same sort of competitive environment as that faced by company CEOs. It is therefore appropriate that they are paid less, though there should probably not be strict pay ratios or upper limits on public sector pay.

Wild recognises, though, that the distinction between public and private is not as clear-cut as is often assumed. There are public sector leadership roles which do face competition, and private sector jobs which nevertheless have a close symbiotic relationship with the public sector. Here it may be appropriate to apply different criteria when determining pay.

One such area is higher education. As so many people now have experience of university, and there is great concern over the levels of debt which graduates have accumulated, it is not surprising that the pay of vice-chancellors and other key staff has attracted considerable (perhaps disproportionate) attention, with the Office for Students now having a virtual power of veto over the pay of senior staff. Rebecca Lowe examines the issues in her chapter.

Lowe points to the considerable range of institutions in the UK higher education sector, and suggests that they should not all be treated the same, whether in pay terms or anything else. She would prefer a formal segmentation of tertiary education as is found in some other countries.

She notes that vice-chancellors are not particularly well paid in relation to their counterparts in the US, Canada or Australia, but points out that the roles in different countries may not be completely equivalent.

Vice-chancellors are, however, paid reasonably well in relation to other staff in their institutions and Lowe argues against letting pay rip at the top end. While UK universities are less directly dependent on the public purse than they used to be, so long as significant government funding supports higher education it is reasonable that we should have special expectations about the way they are run, and how their staff are remunerated.

Policy consequences

Most of these contributors have concentrated on determining the reasons for, and the circumstances in which, governments ought to intervene. Several have drawn attention to possible 'market failures' in the determination of top pay.

However, government interventions always bring with them a corresponding risk of 'government failure', where policies produce unexpected or undesired consequences which in some cases may exacerbate rather than mitigate perceived problems. In a final chapter I point to some of these.

They include the danger that publication of pay ratios may encourage companies to delist and new businesses to register outside the UK, to reduce headcount by outsourcing particularly low-paid jobs, or to reduce the use of performance-related pay for executives.

More radical measures such as imposing worker representation on boards may increase union influence over all aspects of company strategy and thus inhibit rapid change and restructuring, with consequent negative effects on productivity in the long run.

Imposing pay caps or maximum pay ratios will squeeze pay distributions within organisations, with negative effects on the pay of middle management and functional experts. In the case of international businesses it will make it difficult to attract or retain top foreign executives, who currently make up a high proportion of UK companies' leadership.

Within the public sector (and quasi-public sector areas such as charities and universities), a fixed upper limit such as the current £150,000 will, like MPs' pay, be difficult to change for political reasons. Over time it will become more and more out of line with the private sector, leading to recruitment and retention problems.

Finally

Opinions will continue to differ on the appropriateness of high pay in some areas, and also on whether we need government intervention or voluntary change if current pay arrangements are thought to be suboptimal. Our hope is that the various contributions in this book encourage more thoughtful analysis of these issues.

2   WHY FREE MARKETEERS SHOULD WORRY ABOUT EXECUTIVE PAY

Luke Hildyard

Concern about very high levels of executive pay is rarely associated with proponents of unregulated markets. Many of the most prominent critics of top pay practices are animated by worries about income inequality. Free marketeers do not, in general, consider this to be such a problem in and of itself, preferring to focus solely on absolute poverty, rather than relative income differences. And many of the ways of reducing the pay gap between top executives and the wider workforce would involve the type of government intervention of which free market supporters tend to be suspicious.

Thus it has typically been socialists, social democrats and more paternalist conservatives who have generally led the condemnation of the growth in CEO pay packages that has occurred in recent years. In this chapter, however, I will argue that there are very good grounds for advocates of free markets to be worried by prevailing executive pay practices. The pay-setting process is riven with conflicts of interest, poor accountability and lax governance, ultimately leading to something of a stitch-up that enables those in powerful positions to capture sums of money that might otherwise be invested more productively.

Table 1   FTSE-100 CEO to worker pay ratios

Year	CEO pay (£m)	CEO/employee pay ratio[a]	Median UK full-time worker pay (£)
2017	5.66	146	28,758
2016	4.58	128	28,195
2015	5.47	129	27,615
2014	4.36	125	27,215
2013	4.71	137	27,011
2012	4.57	125	26,472
2011	4.43	124	26,095/26,244
2010	4.73	138	25,882
2009	4.22	130	25,806
2008	3.96	128	25,165
2007	3.89	151	24,043
2006	3.31	107	23,367/23,554
2005	3.30	121	22,888
2004	3.09	119	22,011/22,056
2003	2.79	112	21,124
2002	2.60	107	20,376
2001	1.81	75	19,722
2000	1.69	70	18,848
1999	1.23	59	17,803

Sources: High Pay Centre (2015c: 48); High Pay Centre and Chartered Institute of Personnel and Development (2018: 14); Manifest/MM&K (2012: 78); and Office for National Statistics (2017).

[a]Annual change in pay ratios can be affected by changes to the composition of the FTSE 100. For example, the addition of G4S – with a very large number of low-paid employees – caused a significant increase in 2007.

In short, executive pay is more akin to the 'rent seeking' that free market purists condemn than to the productive enterprise they aim to foster. Many of the measures which might potentially put an end to this institutional stitch-up would involve making the 'market' for senior executives freer, more open and more efficient.

Rapid increases in pay for no reason

Public anger at executive pay levels is based around two perceptions. Firstly, that executive pay has increased at a far greater rate than the pay of ordinary workers in recent decades. Secondly, that these executive pay increases have occurred without any corresponding improvement in company performance.

Though often snobbishly dismissed as populist prejudice, these perceptions are in fact largely accurate. Over the past twenty years, the pay of the average FTSE-100 CEO has gone from around 60 times that of their average employee to nearly 150 times in 2017 (Table 1). Compared to the average worker across the UK economy as a whole, CEO pay has risen from about 70 times to nearly 200 times.

Research from the CFA Institute and Lancaster University also found that, while pay for the median FTSE-350 CEO increased by 82 per cent between 2003 and 2014, the median FTSE-350 company generated less than 1 per cent return on invested capital per year. The study concluded that (CFA Society UK 2017: 2):

Despite relentless pressure from regulators and governance reformers over the last two decades to ensure closer alignment between executive pay and performance, evidence of more granular distinction between pay outcomes and fundamental value creation remains negligible.

Similarly, a study by Incomes Data Services, commissioned by the High Pay Centre (2015a), found that increases to each of the different components of typical executive pay awards had greatly outpaced the increases in company performance, as measured according to the performance metrics used in most executive pay packages (Figure 1).

Figure 1   Percentage change in median remuneration of FTSE-350 companies and selected corporate indicators, 2000–2013

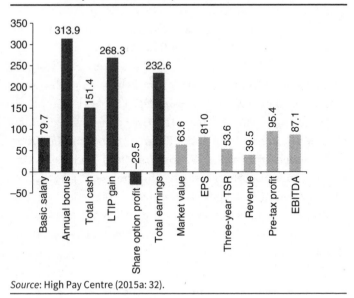

Source: High Pay Centre (2015a: 32).

These independent findings are also endorsed by industry and government analyses. For example, a working group convened by the Investment Association, the trade body for the asset management industry, concluded that 'rising levels of executive pay over the last 15 years have not been in line with the performance of the FTSE over the same period' (Investment Association 2016: 17).

Figure 2   FTSE-100 CEO pay and company value

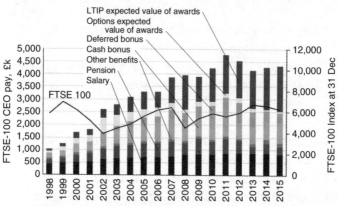

Source: Minerva Analytics (formerly Manifest) Total Renumeration Survey via Department for Business, Energy and Industrial Strategy (2016: 17).

This argument is borne out by Figure 2, taken from the Department for Business, Energy and Industrial Strategy's (2016) Corporate Governance Reform Green Paper. These BEIS figures show the extent to which growth of FTSE-100 CEO pay has outpaced growth of the FTSE-100 index.

The data show that the increasing use of Long-Term Incentive Plans (LTIPs) in particular drove the increase in CEO pay over recent years. LTIPs usually take the form of share awards that pay out varying amounts depending on the company's performance over the coming three- or five-year period.

As Figure 2 suggests, the growth in size and prevalence of LTIPs has done little to raise the value of UK companies. Corporate governance experts have suggested their near-universal use cannot be justified. The UK Investment Association (2016: 12) working group called for more variation in executive pay structures:

> The Working Group's core recommendation is that the market needs to move away from a one-size-fits-all approach to a system where companies have more flexibility to choose the remuneration structure which is most appropriate for their business.

However, since the publication of their report, most companies continue to cling to the LTIP model. The High Pay Centre's research found that in 2017 (the most recent year for which data are available) 82 per cent of FTSE-100 firms paid an LTIP, the same number as in 2016 (High Pay Centre and Chartered Institute of Personnel and Development 2018: 9). The fact that LTIPs pay out for almost every CEO almost every year is particularly indicative of a problem, given that they are supposed to be a performance-related award, used to incentivise exceptional leadership.

The continuing use of LTIPs contributed to an increase in average pay for a FTSE-100 CEO of 24 per cent on the previous year in 2017, while the median pay rose by 11 per cent (ibid.: 14). When increases like these – for the price of a product or service – are sustained for as long as the growth in CEO pay has endured, sensible observers ought to be suspicious.

The myth of the global market and the overstated importance of CEOs

The arguments used to justify these pay increases usually focus on the importance of the decisions taken by CEOs to the performance of companies, and the (positive and negative) effect of these decisions on company value. This can dwarf the amounts paid to CEOs. Companies are supposedly paying the minimum rate necessary in a global market place to attract and retain the people who will take the best decisions

However, evidence for the existence of this 'global market' is limited. A High Pay Centre (2013) study found that fewer than 1 per cent of the world's largest companies had poached their CEO from an international rival. CEO pay is notoriously high in the US, yet it is rare for a UK business leader to be recruited by a US company.

The risk of losing supposedly rare talent by reducing executive pay is much lower than often suggested: 80 per cent of companies in our study had promoted their lead executive from within. Far from needing to pay significant sums of money to convince an external candidate to jump ship, most CEO appointments involve companies taking a chance on a more junior executive and offering them a significant increase in terms of profile, status and responsibility.

Whether ambitious candidates also require vast pay incentives for promotions to more senior roles is questionable. In addition, the preference for internal appointments suggests that familiarity with the particular leadership team, culture, strategy, markets and stakeholders of a company is a key, non-transferable attribute for a CEO. It also implies that the need to use pay increases to retain the services of good executives is overstated – if a company does find itself in that position, it reflects poorly on the quality of its own training and development programmes.

Furthermore, even if it were the case that reducing pay for UK CEOs would result in losing them to international rivals, it is debatable whether this would have much impact on company performance.

Quite apart from the fact that the evidence highlighted in Figure 2 suggests that UK CEOs *haven't* been taking decisions that have greatly increased the value of their companies, the notion that they are the key determinants of company success is hotly contested.

And, as the prominent business leader Philip Hampton notes, the impact of executives at more complex businesses with larger market capitalisation, more internationalised operations and larger workforces may actually be less pronounced than at smaller companies (High Pay Centre 2015a: 10):

The bigger the system, the more the system counts rather than the person at the top of it. ... Sometimes you just get lucky. Perhaps you joined an industry at the right time, maybe you were promoted at the right time, and then the circumstances of your industry suddenly became favourable. Even if you are a half-wit, you are going to do quite well in this situation. So many financial incentives rely on luck, the evolution of markets, rather than on people's contribution.

In other words, the executives of larger companies are only able to personally oversee a much smaller proportion of the business's workings and thus are more dependent on those to whom they delegate. Therefore, it is hard to argue that the business would struggle to cope without them. In fact, the demand for and importance of executives has been greatly exaggerated in order to justify vast pay inflation.

This is particularly true in the case of long-established businesses – most of the publicly listed companies in the UK whose pay is the source of most controversy in this country have histories stretching back many decades and are led by managers and bureaucrats who have worked their way up through the firm and inherited oversight of its existing infrastructures, rather than built them up themselves. They are not entrepreneurs on whom the companies' existences are dependent.

Indeed, free market advocates should be particularly concerned by the extent to which these companies have historically enjoyed and continue to enjoy support from the UK state. The nexus between government and industry is a critical engine of the dominant sectors in the UK listed market. For example, UK mining and oil and gas companies' extensive global operations have been established with significant support from the UK government, and, even in recent years, stories abound relating to UK lobbying of African and South American governments regarding legal issues and exploration permits facing companies including BP, Shell and Rio Tinto.[1]

Similarly, UK defence and manufacturing firms operate almost in partnership with the UK state. The former Foreign Secretary Robin Cook noted that the Chairman of BAE Systems 'appeared to have the key to the garden door to number 10 [Downing Street]' during his tenure.[2] BAE famously benefited from UK government pressure on the Serious Fraud Office to drop an investigation into alleged bribes paid in Saudi Arabia, while more recently it was revealed that it had seconded staff to the Ministry of Defence and a UK government body promoting defence exports.[3] Recent corruption allegations against BAE's competitor Rolls-Royce have also brought into the spotlight financial support for the company from a government agency, the

---

1   Tory ministers lobbied Brazil on behalf of Shell and BP, Government accidentally reveals, *The Independent*, 20 November 2017 (https://www.independent.co.uk/news/uk/politics/tory-ministers-liam-fox-greg-hands-international-trade-lobbied-brazil-bp-shell-oil-environment-a8066236.html); Documents reveal extent of Shell and Rio Tinto lobbying in human rights case, *The Guardian*, 6 April 2014 (https://www.theguardian.com/business/2014/apr/06/shell-rio-tinto-human-rights-nigeria-kiobel).

2   Why is government so close to BAE Systems?, Open Democracy, 24 April 2016 (https://www.opendemocracy.net/uk/andrew-smith/why-is-government-so-close-to-bae-systems).

3   Ibid.

Export Credit Guarantee Department, for deals worth $400 million.[4]

Other instances of so-called crony capitalism include pharmaceuticals companies selling drugs developed from publicly funded research or housebuilders' sales rocketing following the introduction of government subsidies for homebuyers in 2013, enabling Persimmon Chief Executive Jeff Fairburn to bank over £100 million from an incentive payment linked to the company's share price.[5] Bail-outs for banks, and the support that implicit guarantees of bail-outs provide for their stock market value, are a further well-known example.

All told, there is scarcely a major UK company that doesn't significantly benefit in some way from government lobbying, subsidies, public research funding or underwritten guarantees. That is not to say each individual example of state support for private companies is (necessarily) a bad thing. However, it does suggest that paying UK executives as if they were genuine wealth creators and risk-takers who had started their companies from scratch, as opposed to bureaucrats operating at the nexus of corporations and the state, is inappropriate.

---

4   Rolls-Royce faces fresh bribery case, *The Times*, 7 February 2017 (https://www.thetimes.co.uk/article/old-deals-land-rolls-royce-in-hot-water-2bs lft95d).

5   NHS pays pharmaceutical companies millions for drugs developed with taxpayers' money, *The Independent*, 22 October 2017; *The Times*, Taxpayers help to buy £100m bonus for Persimmon boss Jeff Fairburn, 27 November 2017 (https://www.thetimes.co.uk/article/taxpayers-help-to-buy-100m-bon us-for-persimmon-boss-jefffairburn-s55xmz3v8).

So what are the market failures that have allowed this to happen?

The ultimate providers of capital want action on pay

Under the UK's shareholder-policed corporate governance system, the company boards and remuneration committees which set pay are supposed to be accountable to shareholders. These shareholders are expected to exercise effective stewardship, ensuring that governance standards and management practices, including pay, are sufficient to deliver good outcomes.

The money for investment in company shares very often ultimately comes from ordinary people with a pension or savings plan. But, in practice, shareholdings are usually managed by asset managers acting on behalf of individual and institutional investors, who engage with investee companies and vote at their annual general meeting.

The complicated array of intermediaries separating companies, as the ultimate recipient of investment, from the individuals who provide the capital and are the intended beneficiaries of any return, can also include, for example, financial advisers, institutional investment consultants and the different governance, trading and portfolio managers within the asset management firms. This means that the beneficiaries have little influence over the behaviour of the investee companies, which in turn has profound consequences in terms of executive pay.

There can be little doubt that ordinary pension savers would like to see the intermediaries managing their money do more to address excessive top pay in their inves- tee companies. Public opinion surveys consistently show the scale of public disapproval of very high executive pay packages. In recent years polls have shown that two thirds of the public think it inappropriate for CEOs to be paid over £1 million (just 7 per cent took the opposing view in 2012).[6] Similarly, in 2015, 80 per cent of survey respondents felt that gaps between high earners and those on low and middle incomes were too high and should be reduced.[7] More recently, 57 per cent supported (versus 30 per cent who opposed) Jeremy Corbyn's plan to cap executive pay at twenty times the level of the lowest-paid worker.[8]

The merits of capping pay and reducing intra-company pay differences are usually debated in relation to their economic and social impact. However, executive pay also relates on principle to issues of governance, accountability and even morality. The rights associated with share own- ership ought to be asserted in accordance with the wishes and values of the ultimate providers of capital – very often,

6   Public 'want top pay reined in', BBC News, 29 January 2012 (https://www .bbc.co.uk/news/uk-16778264).

7   Briefing 46: Most people think that differences in pay between high and low earners are unfair, Inequality Briefing, 3 October 2014 (http:// inequalitybriefing.org/brief/briefing-46-most-people-think-that-differ ences-in-pay-between-high-and-low).

8   Majority of public support Jeremy Corbyn's plans to cap bosses' salaries, poll suggests, *The Independent*, 14 January 2017 (https://www.independent .co.uk/news/uk/politics/majority-of-public-support-jeremy-corbyn-s -plans-to-cap-bosses-salaries-poll-finds-a7527381.html).

working people with pension plans, insurance policies or savings accounts. There is a very high likelihood that these people share the views of the majority of the cited survey respondents.

However, weak accountability between the different links in the investment chain prevents the providers of capital from exercising due influence over the recipients, including over practices such as executive pay.

Investment beneficiaries lack capacity to influence pay

It is not enough to suggest that because those members of the public that are in some way invested in companies are not beating down the door of their financial adviser or pension fund trustee to do more to challenge executive pay practices, they therefore must find the status quo acceptable. Levels of financial literacy are such that it is likely that all but the most engaged savers (with the most time on their hands) have very little idea how and why their savings are linked to levels of executive pay.

This is borne out by research for the NEST pension provider, finding that many pension savers struggled to understand and explain fairly basic financial concepts such as a 'stock', a 'bond' or an 'interest rate', leading it to conclude that 'a lot of people across all levels of education and achievement don't understand what investment is or how it works' (NEST Corporation 2017: 12).

It is unrealistic to expect these people collectively to assert their share ownership rights in relation to executive pay. This is the crux of the top pay problem, from a free market perspective. In theory, one would expect the investors in a company to retain cost discipline in relation to top pay, and to ensure that the company's wider pay practices are fair and proportionate.

However, most savers lack the understanding or the information to engage with their asset manager (or with the relevant intermediary, such as a pension fund) to create pressure on them to exercise proper stewardship over investee companies in relation to pay (and potentially other issues as well).

Institutional asset owners lack the expertise or engagement to influence asset managers

This market failure could be mitigated if the institutional investors, principally the pension funds through which pension savings are managed, took more of an interest in their asset managers' stewardship on their members' behalf.

However, this is not currently the case. The Financial Conduct Authority (FCA) identifies over 44,000 pension schemes in the UK, but few have signed the Financial Reporting Council's Stewardship Code, committing them to holding their asset managers to account over their stewardship practices. The Code sets out a series of principles on which signatories can state their policy, including monitoring of and engaging with investee companies, and reporting on stewardship practices. For asset managers, this covers their direct engagement with companies. For asset owners – such as pension funds – it involves setting out expectations in this respect of asset managers.

That so few pension funds have signed up to the code perhaps suggests that they are not interested in using the influence they have over the companies in which they are invested, regardless of the views of their members.

The fragmented nature of UK pension funds has also had an important impact on their ability to influence their asset managers. The FCA's Asset Management Market study notes that the large number of smaller schemes reduces the capacity of scheme governance in two ways (Financial Conduct Authority 2016: 70):

- *Investment expertise and resources to spend helping them make investment decisions* – a larger number of schemes means a larger number of governance roles to fill, and fewer resources for each scheme with which to attract appropriately skilled individuals.
- *Greater bargaining power and ability to benefit from economies of scale* – larger investors that form a larger part of the asset manager's client base are better positioned to influence its activities.

The FCA relates the lack of scale to pension funds' inability to secure better value from asset management costs. However, the same problem – scheme governance bodies that lack the time, expertise or financial clout to influence asset managers – also bedevils pension funds' efforts to shape stewardship practices on issues such as executive pay.

Pension funds account for around 44 per cent of the £6.9 trillion worth of assets under management by members of the UK Investment Association (Investment Association 2017). Therefore, they would represent a significant bloc exerting downward pressure on pay – as shareholders and bondholders – if lines of accountability were operating effectively.

Asset managers and remuneration committees are biased and conflicted on pay

Without pressure from their individual clients or from their institutional investors, the asset managers who engage directly with companies and decide how to vote on pay resolutions at AGMs are at best too apathetic and at worst too conflicted to act over top pay of their own accord.

There is evidence to support this hypothesis in numerous studies. The Kay Review (2012: 10) of UK equity markets and long-term decision-making noted the shorter and shorter periods over which shares in companies are traded, making engagement between investment managers and investee companies much less common.

The UK's share ownership market is also increasingly fragmented, meaning that shareholdings are much smaller and more geographically widespread. Just 16 per cent of UK shares were held by overseas investors in 1994, but 54 per cent in the most recent figures.[9] The fragmenta-

9   Ownership of UK quoted shares: 2016, Office for National Statistics, 29 November 2017 (https://www.ons.gov.uk/economy/investmentspensions andtrusts/bulletins/ownershipofukquotedshares/2016).

tion makes it harder for those investors that want to assert their stewardship rights to do so with enough weight to influence the company.

Kay also questioned whether the interposition of intermediaries, with their own business objectives which are not necessarily aligned with companies and beneficiaries (the people who are providing the money for investment), might conflict with the underlying interest of the companies and their beneficiaries (Kay Review 2012: 41).

By the same logic, the personal objectives and biases of the individuals working as investment intermediaries are also potentially distortive of the concerns and interests of their beneficiaries, particularly in relation to executive pay. As Kay noted, pay for investment intermediaries is very high. Surveys have put the pay for a typical portfolio manager – who oversees an asset manager's individual investments – at over £200,000.[10] Other research suggests that average pay at some asset management firms has passed the £1 million mark.[11] Asset managers' pay is subject to many of the same criticisms as executive remuneration.

Despite their generous pay packages (paid for from the costs ultimately accruing to ordinary savers) the majority of investment managers usually fail to 'beat the market'. A study by S&P recently concluded that 86 per cent of 'actively managed' funds failed to achieve better returns than the

---

10 Best and worst paying jobs in finance, Emolument blog (https://www.emol ument.com/career_advice/best_and_worst_paying_jobs_finance).

11 Has fund manager pay gone too far? *Portfolio Adviser*, 18 June 2018 (https:// portfolio-adviser.com/has-fund-manager-pay-gone-too-far/).

FTSE All-Share index in 2016.[12] Over the previous decade, 74 per cent underperformed the market.

Similarly, asset managers are themselves major companies with very highly paid executives. Any move that the asset managers make, as investors, to exert discipline or downward pressure on executive pay is likely to have negative ramifications for the pay of their own executive team.

It is not excessively suspicious to think that the explicit self-interest, as well as the unconscious biases, of asset managers who benefit from a culture of high pay means that their approach to this issue in investee companies does not represent a functional, transparent, efficient market in action. If people working for asset managers justify their own very generous pay packages on the basis of their unique skillset, the value they generate and the need to attract, retain and incentivise key staff, it is highly likely that they would be sympathetic to similar claims made in relation to company executives, however dubious these claims may be, and however they may contravene the views and expectation of their clients.

With the intermediaries in the investment chain unwilling and/or incapable of holding companies to account over their pay practices, the pay-setting process is dependent on the remuneration committee to deliver appropriate outcomes. Unfortunately, such committees are typically riddled with similar biases and conflicts of interest to those of the asset managers that hold them to account.

---

12 Nine in ten popular Isa funds fail to beat the stock market, *Daily Telegraph*, 26 October 2016 (https://www.telegraph.co.uk/investing/funds/90pc-of -popular-isa-funds-fail-to-beat-the-market/).

Like the asset management industry professionals, the business leaders and financiers who populate remuneration committees benefit from a culture of very high top pay. Research from the Trades Union Congress (2015) found that over a third of FTSE-100 companies have executive directors from other companies sitting on their remuneration committee, while 246 out of 383 FTSE-100 remuneration committee members held additional board positions at other companies. Average pay for a remuneration committee member (from all their various positions) was £441,000 (about sixteen times the national average).

This implies that those setting executive pay are personally incentivised to maintain a high market rate for executive roles and are instinctively sympathetic to arguments that also justify their own high pay packages. The fact that executive pay has continued to climb with no obvious justification, the very rare instances in which remuneration committees exercise discretion to revise pay downwards, and the continuing and near universal use of LTIPs as part of CEO pay structures despite extensive expert criticism all suggest that remuneration committees are insufficiently sceptical of prevailing executive pay levels and structures. There are good grounds for thinking that overt self-interest and unconscious bias are at least part of the reason for this.

It is in this aspect of the executive pay-setting process that the charge of rent-seeking most readily applies. Remuneration committees are appointed by and accountable to serving or former executives and other leading professionals from similar backgrounds in major businesses or finance and investment firms. Executives as a group are able to extract disproportionate pay awards from company funds through their dominance of this process, rather than through their productive contribution and enterprise.

Remuneration committees are also typically advised by consultants, who provide market information on the levels and structures of CEO pay, and help to design pay policies. Again, though, this process is blighted by conflicts of interest. It is in the interest of consultants to devise ever more complex pay structures in order to justify their own existence. There is much less work involved (and therefore less need for consultants) in developing a pay package consisting of a basic salary and perhaps some form of share award or profit-sharing arrangement than for a policy involving multiple different incentive plans covering different time periods and 10–12 performance metrics.

The ultimate result of this growing complexity – bolting additional components onto CEO pay awards, with increases in the value of performance-related components to compensate for the fact that executives are likely to apply a discount rate to conditional payments made over a period of years – has been the increases in executive pay discussed in the opening section of this chapter. Any benefits to businesses, their stakeholders or the wider economy are harder to discern.

Why does this matter and what should be done?

I have argued that executive pay has increased without any justification. The ultimate providers of capital – those who own shareholdings in companies and to whom the companies' leadership should be accountable – lack the understanding, information and resources to engage with where their money is invested. Those entrusted with managing their investment are compromised by biases and conflicts of interest. This has resulted in a situation where executive pay is unnecessarily, disproportionately and undeservedly high.

But why should this be important for free market advocates? There are three key reasons. First, the unsatisfactory outcomes resulting from the executive pay-setting process and their high profile will help to create a perception that free markets deliver unsatisfactory outcomes more generally. This is likely to result in anti–free market policies in other policy areas. Second, though headline executive pay awards represent sums of money that are often immaterial to major companies, this does not tell the full story of the costs of rising top pay. The trend of higher CEO pay, with bigger bonuses and more generous share awards made through LTIPs, has probably been reflected in the pay packages for other senior managers across companies.

Since the late 1970s, the share of incomes taken by top earners in the UK has increased from around 6 per cent to about 14 per cent according to the most recent figures.[13] The share going to the top 0.1 per cent has risen from 3 per cent in 1990 to 6 per cent.

A similar increase within companies would represent a substantial shift in spending that could otherwise be

---

13 World Inequality Database, 2014 (https://wid.world/).

used for pay across the wider workforce, for investment in research and innovation or as returns to shareholders. The opportunity costs of rising executive pay have perhaps not been sufficiently discussed or analysed.

Finally, free market advocates should be concerned about CEO pay as a 'canary in the coal mine'. The sensible and sustainable management of UK companies depends on responsible stewardship by investment managers and rigorous accountability between the different intermediaries that form the investment chain.

Executive pay inflation highlights the inadequacies of current stewardship practices and levels of accountability. It raises concerns that negligent and/or self-serving boards and shareholders are not properly holding their companies' management to account – and potentially on other issues as well as pay. This has worrying implications for the productivity and sustainability of the UK's biggest companies and the wider UK economy.

So what is to be done? The High Pay Centre has historically advocated worker representation on boards and remuneration committees as a means of introducing a more challenging, less conflicted perspective into the pay-setting and oversight process. Free market proponents have traditionally been sceptical of stakeholder voices in corporate governance structures, arguing that it could subvert market forces, by making companies accountable to a separate vested interest, as opposed to their customers, or the shareholders who have 'skin in the game' through their investments. There are occasions when it could be in the company's long-term interests to take decisions that would be painful for the workforce, such as making redundancies or reducing expenditure on training and development, and worker directors may make tough but necessary decisions more difficult.

However, worker directors would not have a controlling say, so ought not to be able to prevent such decisions when they are justified by a business case. Furthermore, as we have seen, shareholder oversight of corporate governance is also very often shaped by the vested interests of investment intermediaries. Company workers' interests are closely aligned with the long-term success of the company in that their jobs depend on it.

It should perhaps also be noted that while stakeholder-oriented governance structures with worker participation, as commonly found in continental Europe, are not associated with free markets, there is no reason in principle why they are inconsistent with the low-tax, low-regulation economy that is the long-standing objective of most free market proponents. Indeed, changes to the governance framework under which businesses operate that bring about more equal market-based outcomes are likely to lead to a reduction in taxation and in the regulatory interventions that are traditionally anathema to free marketeers.

Greater transparency is a further measure that could bring about changes in respect of high pay via market mechanisms – the government has recently required companies to publish the pay ratio between their CEO and their median UK employee. More detailed disclosures on pay distribution – showing, for example the amount spent on the pay of the top 1 per cent of earners within the company

– might encourage investors to recognise the opportunity cost of high pay, and exert better stewardship and more effective downward pressure.

Finally, the stewardship process could be made more accountable and democratic by requiring institutional investors to offer some form of voting on company AGM resolutions to their ultimate beneficiaries. The disengagement of savers and low levels of understanding of investment processes mean that this would not be instantly transformative. But it would remind investors of their duties to their underlying clients, and could also engender efforts to better engage consumers with their savings and investments.

These measures are all potential constraints on the unjustifiable executive pay increases that have become too common across UK companies, and are consistent with a pragmatic free market approach to governance and stewardship. The diversion of company resources from already generous executive pay packages to more productive investment would represent the positive economic outcome that free market proponents desire.

By enacting these measures, the government could ensure that an economic system based largely on free market principles maintains popular support at a time when it is being seriously questioned for the first time in a generation.

3 UNDERSTANDING THE 'FACTS' ABOUT TOP PAY

Damien Knight and Harry McCreddie

Introduction

The issue of executive pay, and by this we really mean the pay of directors of listed companies, has been overtaken by concerns which are essentially political, with both a large and small P.

None of the protagonists in this field is innocent. The government is worried about public opinion, while the Opposition maintains its constitutional role of stirring things up. Institutional shareholders are afraid of being accused of poor stewardship. Remuneration committees want to keep below the parapet of 'best practice'. Journalists sell copy (or generate retweets) when they attack 'fat cats' – or indeed remuneration consultants like us.

We argue that journalists and consequently politicians have been persuaded by research and analysis which is fundamentally flawed. They have repeated myths which have served to increase divisions in our society – in particular, the myth that executive remuneration continues to be 'out of control' and the myth that there is no link between executive pay and company performance in large UK listed companies.

Pay granted is not the same thing as pay realised

To understand the research, it is necessary to have some mathematics. The representative of one of the major management institutions announced with pride at a recent conference that he scraped a C in GCE maths, proud because it was a badge of the common man. But this conference was a meeting to receive the results of analytical research on executive pay. To have a valid opinion on executive pay you do need to have mastered some maths – or at least have some logical understanding.

Firstly, there is an important distinction to be made between total remuneration *awarded* (or granted) and total remuneration *realised.* It is all to do with the treatment of long-term incentives such as LTIPs and share options. The inclusion of salary, benefits and annual bonus in the total is the same in both cases.

With total remuneration awarded, the value of long-term incentives included is the fair value or expected value of the share awards at the time of grant. Typically, these values are obtained using a mathematical method based on the Black–Scholes model (Black and Scholes 1973) – in simple cases the Black–Scholes formula itself, in more complicated cases an iterative method such as a Monte Carlo simulation, to which spreadsheets lend themselves wonderfully.

Total remuneration *awarded* is a measure of the generosity of decisions made by the remuneration committee. If remuneration is 'out of control' it will show in the evolution of this figure over time.

With total remuneration *realised*, the value of LTIPs included is the market or cash value at the end of the performance period when any performance conditions have been applied and share prices have (hopefully) gone up. This is typically three years after the date of the award.

Total remuneration realised is the figure to use if we want to see if the eventual executive remuneration 'trousered' by bosses is justified by the performance of the company or explicable by market movements. The decisions the remuneration committee made (level of grant, plan design and performance targets) were taken three years earlier, so total remuneration realised this year is not a good measure for assessing if remuneration is out of control. The government's own Single Total Figure of Remuneration, prescribed in the Directors Reporting Regulations, is a measure of total remuneration realised, so it needs to be viewed with some caution.

What has been happening?

The first thing to say is there is no question that pay for FTSE-100 chief executives has increased hugely and changed greatly in structure over the past forty years (Figure 3). When Damien started remuneration consulting in 1978, chief executives in general had a maximum bonus of 30 per cent of salary and only a handful received share options. LTIPs did not exist. The board usually waited until the union negotiation was concluded before the management award was decided (annual increases were the norm), so as to make sure the management award was no higher than the general settlement.

On the other hand, most senior executives would have had a final salary pension scheme, often at an accrual rate of ¼oths or ⅕₃₅ths. Large salary increases in the final year were not unknown. Non-cash benefits were tax free, so payment of school fees and accommodation costs was a regular perk, as was the provision of a large car (or two) and a driver.

There are many factors that led to a polar change in executive pay – among them the introduction of the UK tax-advantaged share option scheme in 1984 and the reduction of the top rate of taxation to 40 per cent by the Thatcher government in 1988. It was now worth earning a bonus.

Figure 3   FTSE-100 CEO total remuneration: the dot-com boom and pre-2008 were the periods of excess

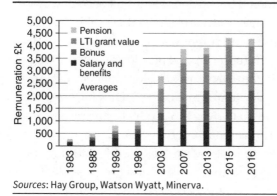

Sources: Hay Group, Watson Wyatt, Minerva.

But more fundamental was the effect of technological change. In 1980 the only effective means of communication was through the management hierarchy and it was common to have twenty layers of management. Chief executives were often not seen as adding much value to the work of their team, so small differentials were the norm.

This changed fundamentally with the advent of distributed computing and mobile telephones. The new generation of top executives believed they personally made a fundamental difference and created huge value. And their boards, too, believed this to be the case and were prepared to pay top dollar for the right person. There was a small recession at the beginning of the 1990s, and as we came out of that the Internet took off, leading to the dot-com boom, which peaked in December 1999.

Increases have flattened out since the banking crisis in 2008. We will see later median figures for more recent years, showing the extent of constraint more accurately.

Lastly the trend in pensions value has been downward as companies have moved to defined contribution plans and to cash in lieu, in response to punitive taxation. With the £10,000 limit to the annual pension allowance we can expect to see top executive pension benefits disappear completely. It is often argued that LTIPs have replaced pensions as the executive saving vehicle, and as a percentage of salary this is probably true.

In Figure 4 we have indexed FTSE-100 CEO pay since 1983 to contrast it with a range of other indices: the FTSE-100, profits and average earnings. All this supports the view that executive pay has outstripped everything. But the 'excess', if that is the right word, happened between 1997 and 2007.

Figure 4   FTSE-100 CEO pay outstripped all other indices

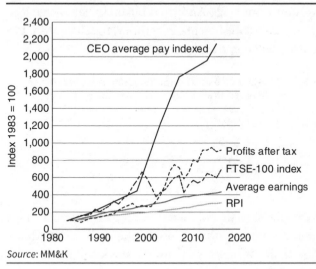

Source: MM&K

How did companies get away with it at the time? The research behind Table 2 was carried out jointly by MM&K and the proxy agency Manifest (previously Minerva) on behalf of the CBI, which produced a report *Getting the Facts Right* in 2012. We studied the 67 FTSE-100 firms in place over the whole period from 2002 to 2010.

The table shows total realised earnings as a percentage of the monetary value of total shareholder returns over the period – that is, the increase in the market capitalisation of each company plus the value of dividends reinvested in the company shares. The median figure is less than half a percent (although the average, not shown here, is just over one per cent). If as a board or a shareholder you believe that your CEO has a significant impact on shareholder returns, why would you worry about how much he or she earns if it is less than 1 per cent? And what business has the government (or the Archbishop of Canterbury) to tell you what to do? But we will come to that.

Table 2   FTSE-100 CEO total remuneration as a percentage of absolute shareholder returns, 2002–10

Lower quartile	0.19%
Median	0.40%
Upper quartile	0.67%

Source: Minerva.

Figure 5 shows in more detail what has happened since the global financial crisis. Here we have shown medians. Unlike mean averages, you cannot stack the medians of each element to reach a median total remuneration, because the median company for one element will not be the same company as the median for another element. So we have shown the median total remuneration as a separate line. You can see that, with this sample, the median total remuneration is higher than the stacked medians for the elements (this means that companies that rank high in one element generally rank lower in another).

But the important conclusion from this graph is that, at the median, awarded remuneration fell after 2011 and remained flat until 2016. The 12 per cent uplift from 2016 to 2017 resulted from a number of highly paid new entrants coming into the FTSE-100 index, causing an increase in the median remuneration that was not due to remuneration committee decisions. The same report from Minerva shows the median increase company by company on a 'same incumbent' basis: it was just 1 per cent. This illustrates well the dangers in interpreting pay statistics.

Figure 5   FTSE-100 CEO total remuneration awarded: since 2011 pay has flattened out

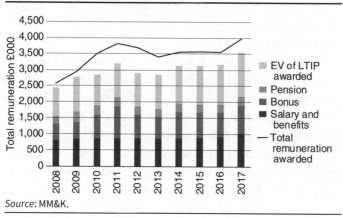

Source: MM&K.

To repeat, 'awarded' remuneration depends on the decisions of the remuneration committee. The long-term incentive element is measured by the fair value at grant and this is the right measure when judging if remuneration committees are 'out of control' in their remuneration decisions.

The unavoidable conclusion is that, for FTSE-100 CEOs, remuneration has been entirely under control, in the majority of cases, since 2011. Between 2014 and 2015 median total remuneration awarded fell slightly. Yet Theresa May promised, when appointed Prime Minister in July 2016, to tackle further the 'problem' of executive pay. The Commons Select

Committee for business produced a report in March 2017 which said that 'levels of pay for those at the top [are] increasing at a rate that vastly exceeds increases for ordinary employees and which seemingly is at odds with the value created in the company' (House of Commons 2017: 37).

The research above shows that the first part of this statement is plainly wrong. But so is the second part, as we can demonstrate.

As we showed earlier, there are two ways of looking at executive remuneration. The figures above are total remuneration *awarded*. However, the government-defined 'Single Total Figure of Remuneration' (the figure in Directors' Remuneration Reports) includes the value of long-term incentive awards at the point that they vest to the individual, i.e. at the end of the performance period, usually three years. The 2018 Minerva survey includes company data up to March 2018, with December 2017 the most common year-end. In the three years to December 2017, the FTSE-100 index increased from 6,566 to 7,688, an increase of 17 per cent. It is not surprising that in the latest year, the Single Total Figure increased by 6 per cent at the median. It has nothing to do with remuneration committees awarding excessive amounts but everything to do with the increase in share prices. On paper, at least, the value of FTSE-100 companies increased by 17 per cent, which gives the lie to the second part of the Select Committee's belief 'which seemingly is at odds with the value created in the company'. The value increase may be due to market sentiment rather than executive performance, but the statement is still wrong.

And this is where the mischief starts. The High Pay Centre[1] also runs a survey along the lines of the Minerva survey: it predictably tells a story of executive excess. Their headline is 'CEO mean pay has increased by 23%'. They should never report mean pay as it is grossly distorted by excessive pay in a few companies (e.g. Persimmon's £47 million to then-CEO Jeff Fairburn, including a £45 million realised LTIP). Hidden in a paragraph further down their report is an admission that the median increase is only 6 per cent (the same as the Minerva figure – not surprising as it is taken from the same annual reports). But the newspapers see 23 per cent and so, we are afraid, does the Commons Select Committee. Thus the 'fat cat' story is perpetuated, although companies have really been exercising restraint for the past ten years.

Flawed research and interpretation

Which brings us to the role of flawed research and its interpretation. But first a quick maths quiz, which points to some of the common errors made by non-mathematicians interpreting pay data.

Question 1

A cosmetic company employs two sales teams of three people each.

---

1   The High Pay Centre is the successor to the High Pay Commission, a creation of the left-wing Compass campaigning group.

In the first year the London team is very successful. All three receive a salary of £40k and a £25k bonus. The Manchester team doesn't do as well and each member just receives the £40k salary and no bonus.

In the second year, the position is reversed. Manchester gets £40k and a £25k bonus each, while the London team simply gets the £40k basic salary.

What is the average percentage increase in earnings?

The (perhaps counter-intuitive) answer is 12 per cent. Not zero, because the increase for each member of the Manchester team is off a lower figure than the decrease in the London figure, so their percentage increase is greater than the London team's percentage fall. You can just see the headline in *Cosmetic World Weekly*: 'Sales team pay increases by 12 per cent when shop floor pay is frozen.' This distortion is always present when looking at average *increases*. The percentage increase in the average *earnings* (as opposed to the average increase) *is* zero.

Question 2

In 2010, in each of 88 FTSE-100 companies executive director total remuneration *realised* increased by 8 per cent; total remuneration *awarded* increased by 2 per cent in these companies.

In the other twelve companies, executive director total remuneration *realised* increased by 390 per cent (because no LTIPs or ESOs had vested the previous year).

What was the median increase in remuneration realised, and what was the median increase awarded?

What was the average increase in remuneration realised?

This is the picture that emerged in the financial years up to March 2011. The numbers are simplified, but the answers are: median *realised*, 8 per cent; median *awarded*, 2 per cent. But the effect of the twelve companies on the *average* increase in realised remuneration (including the 'cosmetic salesman' effect from Question 1) resulted in an *average* increase of 49 per cent for FTSE-100 executive directors. The research firm, Incomes Data Services, which used to publish an annual analysis of increases, issued a press release headlining this second figure: 'FTSE 100 directors award themselves a 49 percent increase in pay.'

There was a national outcry from which the reputation of big company directors has never recovered. David Cameron waded in, saying he found the figure 'very disturbing'. The then Archbishop of Canterbury (Rowan Williams) condemned the greed of the executives. All this happened at the time Vince Cable, then Business Secretary, was consulting on the new reporting regulations.

Despite this condemnation, both the government and the investor institutions were repeating the philosophy that they had no problem with high pay, provided it was justified by corporate performance. This had always been the position of those supporting free markets.

We believe that this position has changed – that there is now a common acceptance that executive pay is too high *full stop*, and it is the disparity between top pay and average pay that is socially divisive. Few people now dare repeat the old free market philosophy. This marks a fundamental shift from shareholder primacy to governance based on 'social justice' principles.

The High Pay Centre has had a seminal role in this change. It commissioned research by the now-defunct IDS Remuneration Services, looking at the top 350 companies. The IDS report[2] was launched at a public meeting of the High Pay Centre in October 2014. Its conclusion was that 'based on the research presented here', increases in all the key elements of FTSE 350 directors' remuneration had far outstripped a range of corporate metrics and there was little discernible link between executive earnings and corporate performance. A distinguished panel received the research. This included *Financial Times* leader writer John Plender, who observed that 'we always suspected that was the case and I am not surprised'. The launch was attended by several journalists and the conclusion made headlines. The lack of a link between executive earnings and corporate performance is now received wisdom, repeated endlessly by journalists, politicians and trade unions, and as seen above, by the Commons Select Committee.

Unfortunately, the analysis was seriously flawed and its conclusions were totally incorrect. To illustrate why, here is Question 3 in our maths test.

---

2 New High Pay Centre report: Performance-related pay is nothing of the sort, High Pay Centre, 28 October 2014 (http://highpaycentre.org/pubs/new-high-pay-centre-report-performance-related-pay-is-nothing-of-the-sort).

Question 3

In a sample of six companies, every CEO is paid a bonus based on a pure percentage of operating profits (OP). The percentage share is different in each company. The results of their bonus calculations are given in Table 3.

Table 3   Bonus calculation

	Company A	Company B	Company C	Company D	Company E
CEO profit share	0.5%	2%	4%	5%	10%
OP £000	Bonus £000				
0	0	0	0	0	0
1,000	5	20	40	50	100
5,000	25	100	200	250	500
10,000	50	200	400	500	1,000
15,000	75	300	600	750	1,500

What is the correlation between CEO bonus and performance across the whole group?

It is clear that the correlation between operating profits and bonus is 100 per cent for each of the companies in the set. R squared in each case is 100 per cent. We can say the bonus is completely linked to performance and this is true of each of the five companies. But R squared for a regression analysis of the whole set drops to 38 per cent – not a good fit. Why is this?

The reason can be seen in the combined scattergram below. Because each company has a different profit share percentage, the points are all over the place and the regression analysis is not a good explainer of differences in bonus (Figure 6).

Figure 6   Bonus and performance across the sample

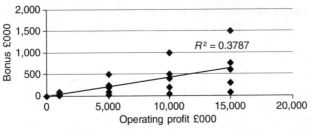

Our scattergram is the result of combining five companies all with a single profit measure. The IDS analysis for the High Pay Centre carried out the same analysis for a sample of 350 companies in the FTSE 100 and FTSE 250. As well as the sheer number of companies, most of them would have had a range of measures of which profit would be only one. Not surprisingly they got a very low R squared (1.3 per cent) and concluded there was no link between bonus and profit. But, as in our example, there could in theory have been a perfect link in each individual company. The IDS analysis as it stands could not reject such a hypothesis.

If studies are going to look at the link between pay and company performance, in order to test a hypothesis that pay is not explained by performance, it is essential that companies are looked at individually and tested in the light of their own stated measures of performance. Now it is perfectly legitimate to debate the measures chosen by an individual company and whether they indicate success as perceived by shareholders or other stakeholders. But it is not legitimate to look for correlations with standard measures across 350 companies at the same time.

But the journalists bought the story, of course, as it fed into the narrative that they 'always suspected' was the case.

Conclusion

Our view is that poor research and analysis has done more damage to social cohesion than the companies themselves have done by paying their top executives highly. It has created a bandwagon onto which the historical champions of free market capitalism – Tory governments, institutional investors, non-executive directors and the financial press – have all felt obliged to clamber.

We are glad to say that, as things have turned out, the government has been sensible in the new corporate governance measures it has so far introduced. The year 2018 was the culmination of a journey that began with a Green Paper and consultation in November 2016. In 2018 the Financial Reporting Council issued a new edition of the UK Corporate Governance Code and it is revising the Stewardship Code for institutional investors. It has been sponsoring the new governance principles for large private companies – the 'Wates Principles' (Financial Reporting Council 2018). BEIS introduced significant new disclosure regulations covering the CEO pay ratio, reporting on engagement with various stakeholders and additional remuneration reporting requirements. The Investment Association has introduced, on the government's instigation, the 'name and shame' register of AGM resolutions that fail to receive 80 per cent or more of votes.

To achieve change in relation to supposed 'fat cat' pay, the government, and the FRC under its direction, has focused on improving disclosure as a change lever and has avoided bringing in specific prescriptions in remuneration policy. This is encouraging. But we have not seen the end of lobbying and in the event of a change of government the Labour Party has promised a cap on total remuneration. It makes it doubly important that all parties involved in policy-making are working with honest and rigorous statistics – and that they brush up their basic maths.

4 THE RIGHTS AND WRONGS OF CEO PAY

Alex Edmans

Introduction

Few business topics capture the public's interest – and anger – as CEO pay. Indeed, a major reason why executives carried little weight in the Brexit referendum may have been the belief that our business leaders are overpaid crooks.

But does perception match reality? The public's view is largely shaped by what the media reports. And the media have the incentive to report the most egregious cases – of CEOs being paid millions despite poor performance – because they make for good stories. There might be thousands of cases where pay is fair, which never get reported. This is similar to how views on immigration (another topic arguably misunderstood in the referendum) may be skewed by newspapers only reporting stories of benefit-scrounging immigrants, when there are millions of others working hard and paying taxes.

Executive pay should definitely be reformed, and I've argued for reform on many occasions. But, just as a doctor needs to make an accurate diagnosis before prescribing the treatment, we need to start with the facts before proposing any reform. What are the areas in most serious need of remedy, and what are the ones that are working well? We want to avoid amputating a limb that's actually healthy. Most of what we think we know about executive pay is actually untrue, because it's based on flimsy research, coupled with confirmation bias – the willingness to accept half-baked evidence because it confirms what we would like to be true (the idea that executives are crooks).

Some common myths about CEO pay

CEOs are unaccountable for poor performance

This myth is based on the view that salaries and bonuses are relatively insensitive to performance, propagated in part by a well-cited study[1] by MSCI. But changes in salaries and bonuses are only a very small part of a CEO's overall incentives. The biggest component is his or her stock and options holdings. Some studies take into account stock and options granted this year, but we must also take into account *all* stock and options granted in previous years. What matters is *wealth*-performance sensitivity, not *pay*-performance sensitivity – i.e. the sensitivity of the CEO's entire wealth to performance. (I have discussed other issues with the MSCI study elsewhere.[2])

---

1 Are CEOs paid for performance?, Your SRI (http://info.msci.com/are-ceos -paid-for-performance).

2 Why the MSCI study does NOT show that equity incentives backfire, Access to Finance blog (http://alexedmans.com/why-the-msci-study -does-not-show-that-equity-incentives-backfire/).

As a simple example, Steve Jobs was famously paid $1 a year at Apple, regardless of performance. Does this mean he didn't care about performance? Clearly not, because he had billions of his own wealth invested in the company's stock. Taking this into account, the median S&P 500 CEO loses $6.7 million when the stock price falls by just 10 per cent (Edmans et al. 2017). Moving to the UK, PwC calculates that this figure is £650,000 for the median FTSE-100 CEO.[3] It's smaller, but still substantial, and if anything the comparison might suggest that UK CEOs need more equity compensation, not less as many politicians claim.

Sir Vince Cable, the leader of the Liberal Democrat party and the former Secretary of State for Business, Innovation and Skills, has frequently quoted unpublished, non-peer-reviewed studies claiming that CEOs are not punished for poor performance. But these studies simply do not measure incentives properly. They only study salaries and bonuses and ignore the CEO's shareholdings.

CEOs are overpaid because shareholders are powerless

The myth is that pay is designed by directors who are in the CEO's pocket, and rubber-stamp excessively generous packages. Shareholders are too small for directors to listen to them.

---

3   Executive pay in a world of truthiness, PwC (https://www.pwc.co.uk/services/human-resource-services/insights/demystifying-executive-pay/executive-pay-in-a-world-of-truthiness.html).

So what happens when shareholders *can* run the show? Evidence shows that, when private equity firms and hedge funds take large stakes in firms, they're not afraid to make major changes. They improve operating performance, increase innovation, and even fire the CEO in many cases. But they very rarely cut the CEO's pay. While large investors see many things to fix in a firm, the level of pay doesn't seem to be one of them.

Incentive pay doesn't work

There are various studies that show that incentives don't work for many jobs. This is because performance measures only capture one dimension of performance. For example, paying teachers based on test results may encourage them to teach-to-the-test. But none of these studies are on CEOs. For CEOs, there is an almost all-encompassing performance measure – the stock price. In the long run (always an important caveat), the stock price reflects all CEO actions, including employee satisfaction, customer satisfaction, environmental stewardship, and patent citations.

Indeed, a comprehensive study (von Lilienfield-Toal and Ruenzi 2014) finds that CEOs with high stock ownership outperform those with low share ownership by 4–10 per cent per year. Moreover, further tests suggest that it's share ownership that causes outperformance, rather than CEOs who predict that their stock will outperform being more willing to accept shares in the first place.

High pay inequality causes poor performance

Even if the level of pay is too small compared to firm value to have a large direct effect – a point we'll revisit later – perhaps it has an important indirect effect through affecting morale? But a recent study (Mueller et al. 2017) finds that, in the UK, firms with higher within-firm pay inequality exhibit higher operating performance and higher long-run shareholder returns. Faleye et al. (2013) find a similar positive link between pay ratios and performance in the US.

While the book *The Spirit Level* (Wilkinson and Pickett 2009) is frequently quoted as showing that inequality causes negative outcomes, the statistical analysis is extremely weak. Most of the analysis regresses an outcome variable (e.g. happiness, obesity) on inequality with no controls at all. There are very many other potential determinants of the outcome variables (e.g. the average level of income, rather than inequality) which are ignored. Such an analysis, with no control variables, would never get through peer review at even a low-tier academic journal, but has been accepted uncritically by people who are eager to believe the findings.

Binding say-on-pay is better than advisory say-on-pay

Theresa May initially advocated moving from advisory say-on-pay to binding say-on-pay. It certainly sounds tougher. But a careful study of eleven countries (Correa and Lel 2016) has found that advisory say-on-pay has proven more effective than binding say-on-pay in both decreasing the level of pay and increasing its sensitivity to performance.

There are clearly many dimensions of the pay debate for which facts are irrelevant. For example, whether pay should be driven by efficiency or equality is a subjective topic about which reasonable people can disagree. And even given a set of facts, reasonable people can disagree on how to interpret them. But we should at least start the discussion with facts, rather than myths and hunches. Companies cannot launch a new drug without providing evidence of its safety and effectiveness. In contrast, politicians and policymakers feel they can make calls for reform without even attempting to back them up with evidence.

We must stop obsessing over CEO pay ratios

In 2017, the average S&P 500 CEO in the US earned 361 times the pay of the median worker.[4] The median UK FTSE-100 CEO earned 137 times more (High Pay Centre and Chartered Institute of Personnel and Development 2018). These figures are the number one piece of evidence that executive pay is excessive and the number one statistic that advocates of pay reform argue should be fixed. Accordingly, both the UK and US are mandating pay disclosure. It is hoped that such disclosure will shame firms into lowering the ratio; investors, customers and employees can boycott firms with overpaid bosses.

---

4   Executive Paywatch, AFL-CIO (https://aflcio.org/paywatch).

I strongly believe that executive pay should be reformed. My own research demonstrates the substantial benefits to firms of treating their workers fairly. However, disclosure of pay ratios may have unintended consequences that actually end up hurting workers. A CEO wishing to improve the ratio may outsource low-paid jobs, avoid employing part-time workers or invest in automation rather than labour. He or she may raise workers' salaries but slash other benefits: pay is only one dimension of what a firm provides. Research shows that, after salary reaches a certain (relatively low) level, workers may place a higher value on non-wage benefits, such as on-the-job training, flexible working conditions and opportunities for advancement. Indeed, a high pay ratio can indicate promotion opportunities, which motivate rather than demotivate workers. A snapshot measure of a worker's current pay is a poor substitute for their career pay within the firm.

The pay ratio is also a misleading statistic because CEOs and workers operate in very different markets, so there is no reason for their pay to be linked – just as a solo singer's pay bears no relation to a bassist's pay. This consideration explains why CEO pay has risen much more than worker pay. As an analogy, Wayne Rooney was not clearly more talented than Bobby Charlton, but he was paid far more because football had become a much bigger, more global industry by the time he was playing.

Just as the football industry has become bigger, so have firms (also as a result of the global marketplace), and so it is worth paying top dollar for top talent. Even if the best player is only slightly better than the next-best player at that position, the slight difference can have a huge effect on the team's fortunes and revenues.

Median firm size in the FTSE 100 today is £9 billion. Thus, even if a CEO contributes only 1 per cent more to firm value than the next-best alternative, this contribution is worth £90 million – much higher than the £4 million median salary. Gabaix and Landier (2008) show that the sixfold increase in CEO pay between 1980 and 2003 can be fully explained by the sixfold increase in firm size.

The same argument does not apply to average workers. A CEO's actions are scalable. For example, if the CEO improves corporate culture, it can be rolled out firm-wide, and thus has a larger effect in a larger firm. One per cent is £10 million in a £1 billion firm, but £90 million in a £9 billion firm. In contrast, most employees' actions are less scalable. An engineer who has the capacity to service ten machines creates, say, £50,000 of value regardless of whether the firm has 100 or 1,000 machines. In short, CEOs and employees compete in very different markets, one that scales with firm size and one that scales less.

In addition to creating misleading comparisons between firms of different size, the pay ratio is not comparable across different industries. It is lower in investment banks than supermarkets – but that's because mid-level bankers are paid pretty well rather than because banking executives are paid poorly. Even within an industry, average pay depends on which countries a firm operates in and its mix of capital and labour.

I fully share the aim behind revealing pay ratios, which is to consider other stakeholders. But this aim is best achieved by encouraging CEOs to increase the pie for all, rather than shrinking CEOs' share of the pie. The website of the AFL-CIO, the largest federation of trade unions in the US, implies that high CEO pay means 'more for them, less for us'. But a salary of £4 million is less than 0.05 per cent of a £9 billion firm value. The amount of the pie that can be redistributed to other stakeholders by reducing CEO pay is tiny. Instead, what matters for the size of the pie isn't the level of pay, but the incentives that it provides to CEOs: as Jensen and Murphy (1990) famously argued: 'It's not how much you pay, but how'. The best way to encourage CEOs to consider all stakeholders is to link pay to the long-run stock price. For example, research shows that improving employee satisfaction increases long-run stock returns by 2.3–3.8 per cent per year, but takes four to five years to fully show up in the stock price (Edmans 2011, 2012). Extending the vesting horizon from three years to six years will encourage CEOs to invest in employee satisfaction. It is better to focus on reforms that create 2.3–3.8 per cent of firm value, not 0.05 per cent.

Indeed, a study by Flammer and Bansal (2016) shows that granting CEOs long-term incentives has a positive causal effect on both firm value and operating performance. The channel is that it leads CEOs to increase both innovation and stewardship of customers, the environment, society, and, in particular, employees. This makes sense – such investments take a long time to pay off, so only far-sighted CEOs will undertake them. Thus, if we want companies to be more innovative and purposeful, lengthening horizons is much more effective than cutting pay.

What's wrong with LTIPs?

Pay reform should thus focus not on the level of pay, but its structure. Current pay schemes are complex, opaque, and encourage short-termism. Take, for example, the case of BP's CEO Bob Dudley: how did he get paid £14 million in 2015, despite the stock price falling by over 15 per cent?

Figure 7   LTIP payoff

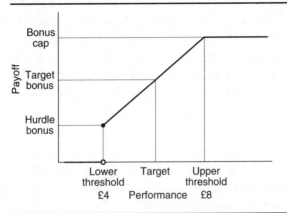

It was the result of his Long-Term Incentive Plan (LTIP). LTIPs pay the executive according to multiple perfor-mance measures – for example, stock price, profitability and sales growth – at the end of an evaluation period (say, three years). For each measure, there's a lower threshold (say, a stock price of £4) that the executive must beat for the LTIP to pay off, as Figure 7 illustrates. The value of the LTIP rises with further increases above £4, before maxing out at a higher threshold (say, £8).

The philosophy behind LTIPs is sound – to link pay to future performance. But it does so in a needlessly complicated way that allows for gaming and fudging.

Let's start with gaming. Despite the name, evidence shows that 'long-term' incentive plans lead to short-termism as the end of the evaluation period approaches. If the stock price is just below £4, the CEO may cut R&D, to boost earnings and get the short-term stock price over the hurdle. The CEO might also gamble. If the gamble fails, the stock price falls to £3, but the LTIP wouldn't have paid off anyway, so the downside is limited. If the gamble succeeds, the stock price rises to £5, and the CEO cashes in. Effectively, the LTIP gives a one-way bet. And the problems aren't limited to the bottom end. If the stock price is just above £8, there is no further upside. Rather than innovating, the executive may coast and become excessively conservative.

These thresholds are crazy. Society loses if firm performance is disastrous (£3) rather than bad (£4). And society gains if firm performance is great (£9) rather than good (£8). But, for the LTIP, there's no difference between disastrous and bad, or between great and good.

Turning to fudging, there is a huge amount of ambiguity on how to design an LTIP.

What performance metrics should be used? Should there be non-financial measures, e.g. treatment of workers? But if so, any measure will be incomplete, and encourage focus only on the measure being rewarded. For example, measuring worker pay won't capture working conditions.

How do we weight the measures? Should it be 52 per cent on the stock price, 27 per cent on profitability, and 21 per cent on sales growth? Bob Dudley received his £14 million, despite the stock price fall, as a result of heavy weighting on the safety and profit targets. Even worse, the weightings are sometimes changed after the fact, to overweight the dimension that the executive performs best on.

How do we choose the thresholds? There's no clear reason for £4, £8 or any number. In practice, the lower threshold is often easy to hit, leading to perceptions of unfairness – why should executives get a bonus for average performance, when ordinary workers don't? Moreover, the thresholds are sometimes lowered if there's a bad external shock (in BP's case, an oil price decline) – but they are not adjusted upwards when good luck happens – again leading to a one-way bet.

Just pay them with shares! Simplicity, transparency and sustainability

What's the solution? Corporations should get rid of LTIPs and other bonuses, and move towards paying the CEO in cash and shares (with a long holding period). This satisfies three principles.

Simplicity. Make it simple. You don't need to choose particular measures, weightings or thresholds, and so the CEO doesn't divert attention to gaming the system. It's simpler than the alternative of giving executives cash and making them buy shares (even though it reaches the same outcome) as CEOs can game when they buy the shares (e.g. by releasing bad news to depress the stock price just before buying).

Transparency. While it's very difficult to value an LTIP, the value of stock is unambiguous. We know how much the CEO gets paid, and under what circumstances – according to the long-term stock price.

Sustainability. It leads to sustainable performance. As discussed earlier, while the short-term stock price can be manipulated, the long-run stock price captures stakeholder value as well as shareholder value, and granting long-term equity has a positive *causal* effect on future profitability, innovation and stakeholder relations.

Note such shares would not be given for free; they would be accompanied by a reduction in cash salary. To repeat, this is superior to paying CEOs in cash and making them buy shares, as they might strategically time the purchase of their shares.

The idea of de-emphasising LTIPs and increasing long-vesting equity was also recommended by the House of Commons Business, Energy and Industrial Strategy Select Committee on Corporate Governance (2017), the Norwegian Sovereign Wealth Fund (Norge Bank 2017), the UK government in a Green Paper on Corporate Governance Reform (2016) and the Purposeful Company Executive Remuneration Report (2017). In 2018, the Weir Group became the first FTSE-350 company to replace LTIPs with long-vesting equity with support from both proxy advisors.

A very important advantage of shares is that they can be given to all employees as well. Giving shares to all employees will allow them all to – quite literally – share in the firm's success that they all helped create.

This will help address fairness concerns. If the firm succeeds, why should only executives benefit? Employees contributed to the firm's success as well. If they are given shares, they will benefit too. CEOs can't gain without employees gaining also. By contrast, if CEOs get LTIPs while workers get shares, the LTIP might pay off even if the stock price falls, leading to concerns of 'one rule for them, another rule for us'. Evidence shows that broad-based equity plans improve performance, perhaps due to a team mentality.

Conclusion

In sum, let's move away from the pie-splitting mentality of pay ratios, and towards the pie-enlarging mindset of value creation. Rather than bringing the CEO's pay down, reform should incentivise the CEO to bring everyone else's up.

5 WHAT CONCLUSIONS CAN WE DRAW FROM INTERNATIONAL COMPARISONS OF CORPORATE GOVERNANCE AND EXECUTIVE PAY?

Vicky Pryce

In a world where large multinationals dominate and can move money, headquarters and production around at will, keeping track of developments and being able to regulate them have now become too difficult for a single country to achieve on its own. Coordination in approach is needed to avoid arbitraging taking place, which can be destabilising. We have seen areas where countries working together helps, such as in the imposition of sanctions, being tougher on controls to prevent money laundering, greater checks on illegal or unexplained capital flows and attempts by Western institutions such as the OECD to ensure that multinational firms, especially those in the technology sector, are paying their fair share of tax in the country where revenues are earned. The EU competition authorities are becoming increasingly effective at using competition policy against internet giants and other dominant international players.

Yet so far there is very little coordination to mitigate the sometimes astronomical pay awards for top executives in countries such as the UK and the US, despite increasing shareholder and popular discontent. Yes, we have seen a rise in shareholder activism and some countries have legislated to give increased powers to block remuneration committees' recommendations. But we are far from an international consensus on executive pay – except perhaps in such small ways as the EU's attempts to restrict bonuses in the financial sector. It certainly looks from the outside like a failure of corporate governance, particularly of multinational firms, despite the increase in awareness and publicity and the increased reporting that now exists through pressure from the corporate social responsibility movement.

How the debate has evolved

There is no doubt that perceptions have changed. With accelerated globalisation the stakes seem to have become much higher.

The issue has been around for some time and positions have been hotly contested. An important starting point is the work of Michael Jensen and Kevin Murphy (1990). These authors questioned whether the perception that CEOs were overpaid was correct. In their view CEOs were rather being *under*paid by historical standards. The authors agreed that compensation policy was a crucial factor in a company's success but argued that protests from the business press, unions and politicians intimidated board members, who were reluctant to link pay to performance as this might produce highly visible rewards for top performers. The corollary was that they were also reluctant to impose meaningful financial penalties for underperformance and took refuge in risk-averse bureaucratic compensation systems. Jensen and Murphy concluded that average CEO pay would 'be higher if the relation between pay and performance were stronger' and that 'managers would have greater incentives to find creative ways to enhance corporate performance' as a consequence.

Much more aggressive performance-related pay has certainly been implemented since then and, although it may have flushed out some bad managers, the results haven't always been pretty to watch. They have often led to perverse behaviour by CEOs and other executives, apparently focused on improving their own rewards rather than the firm's long-term sustainability – the classic principal/agent problem.

What do the facts tell us about international variations in executive pay?

A common belief in Britain is that most instances of very high pay arise in the US and the UK, which have been run on what is (usually disparagingly) known as the 'Anglo-Saxon' or 'neoliberal' economic model. What is the evidence? A Bloomberg report in November 2016[1] looked at

---

1   The best and worst countries to be a rich CEO, Bloomberg, 25 November 2016 (https://www.bloomberg.com/professional/blog/best-worst-countries-rich-ceo/).

25 of the world's largest economies and compared what CEOs of listed firms on the main benchmark index of each country received, and then compared that with the average CEO pay across the 25 countries surveyed, which was $6.5 million.

This showed that the US came top in that year with an average payment of $16.95 million for a CEO of companies listed on the S&P 500. This was 2.6 times that of the average CEO pay of all the countries on the list. Switzerland came second – at 1.6 times the average. Then the UK at an average of $9.61 million for CEOs of companies on the FTSE 100, followed by Canada and the Netherlands. But rather surprisingly Germany came in seventh, with an average CEO pay of companies listed on the Dax 30 of $8.36 million, only around $1 million dollars less than the UK.

Another way of looking at the issue is to focus on what top executive pay is in relation to average per capita income in the country in question. This is illustrated in Table 4. On this metric South Africa and India were the most generously compensated countries despite scoring low in absolute terms, showing the degree of inequality that exists in those countries. However, on this measure the US was still very high in third place and the UK in fourth. Canada and Switzerland slipped to fifth and sixth but Germany was there again in seventh place.

Germany's high ranking may come as a shock. We are accustomed to thinking that large German firms, subject to a supervisory board where worker representatives sit, should be an example of transparency, perceived fairness and moderation. But we forget how open and externally focused big German firms are and how much they trade with the rest of the world. They compete for top people like every other player in global markets. Bill McDermott is an American who heads SAP, Europe's largest technology firm. In 2017 he was the highest-paid CEO in Germany,[2] reportedly having a package worth some €21.8 million, including what were termed 'retention share units'. Like other large multinational firms, SAP can probably justify this to shareholders in terms of needing to offer a package attractive enough to secure and retain international talent.

Other highly paid German CEOs covered in the Bloomberg figures include the boss of the chemicals firm BASF and the CEO of the electronics firm Siemens. Then there is the erstwhile CEO of Volkswagen, Matthias Muller, ousted in April 2018 after his company was heavily involved in and fined for the 'Dieselgate' scandal,[3] which put the spotlight on German company corporate governance and firm behaviour. The CEO of Daimler, Dieter Zetsche, who has had to recall thousands of Mercedes vans and explain himself to the transport minister in Berlin, is another top earner. There are also reports of deepening EU investigations into collusion of the main car makers BMW, Daimler and Volkswagen.

---

2   German executive pay gets supersized, *Handelsblatt*, 15 March 2018 (https://global.handelsblatt.com/companies/german-executive-pay-gets -supersized-898574).

3   Billions of euros in fines are possible if diesel emission tests were inaccurate, *Handelsblatt*, 28 May 2018 (https://global.handelsblatt.com/com panies/dieselgate-mercedes-benz-diesel-recall-puts-daimler-boss-ceo -dieter-zetsche-in-the-hot-seat-928165).

Table 4   Global CEO pay-to-average income ratio, 2016

Rank	Economy	Pay ratio	CEO pay $million, latest filing	GDP p.c. PPP 2015/16 ($)
1	S. Africa	514.40	7.14	13,194
2	India	483.06	3.10	6,423
3	US	298.98	16.95	56,689
4	UK	228.70	9.61	42,006
5	Canada	202.98	9.32	45,921
6	Switzerland	179.34	10.58	59,011
7	Germany	175.65	8.36	47,582
8	Spain	172.42	6.15	35,656
9	Netherlands	172.32	8.66	50,235
10	Israel	119.42	4.11	34,444
11	S. Korea	113.98	4.25	37,280
12	Australia	113.07	5.45	48,225
13	Norway	100.99	6.96	68,944
14	Denmark	82.07	3.79	46,163
15	Sweden	74.95	3.67	48,938
16	France	67.65	2.84	41,930
17	Hong Kong	66.20	3.81	57,487
18	Malaysia	66.03	1.76	26,723
19	Singapore	64.89	5.60	86,232
20	Japan	62.33	2.40	38,518
21	Finland	61.20	2.54	41,461
22	Austria	46.57	2.21	47,421
23	China	43.00	0.64	14,882
24	Poland	23.94	0.65	27,107
25	Thailand	3.94	0.06	16,483

Source: Bloomberg.

The figures in Table 4, and other data, suggest that Asian countries' CEO pay has in some cases risen to parity with the West. And it may be that in countries such as China, where stock options offered by public companies remain limited, there may be some serious under-recording or under-reporting, as bonuses are often hidden. There may also be unreported payments for on-duty consumption such as food and travel and office expenses, which can often substantially increase overall compensation levels.[4]

It is, however, difficult to generalise from these figures about whether the overall remuneration of CEOs is excessive in some countries and too low in others, and what the 'best' system should be. Differences in effective pay may in the end simply reflect different cultures rather than being a sign of widely differing CEO capabilities. Before the German elections in September 2017, the socialist SPD was working to introduce a bill taxing CEO bonuses more heavily and reducing tax deductibility on pension contributions, as well as allowing shareholders to set CEO salaries as a multiple of average pay in the firm. The supervisory board, which includes worker representatives in big firms, would also have the right to reduce executive pay in the cases of poor performance or misconduct.[5] The SPD is currently in power as part of the CDU/SPD coalition after many months of

4   Shrouded in mystery: Chinese executive compensation and the numbers behind the numbers, Knowledge@Wharton blog, 14 May 2012 (http://knowledge.wharton.upenn.edu/article/shrouded-in-mystery-chinese-executive-compensation-and-the-numbers-behind-the-numbers/).

5   Focus on executive pay expected to sharpen as German poll looms, *Financial Times*, 11 April 2017 (https://www.ft.com/content/f1733428-157c-11e7-b0c1-37e417ee6c76).

post-election negotiations and it remains to be seen how many of its proposals will survive. But German politicians will undoubtedly have to respond to ongoing concern over CEO pay packages: despite in most cases remaining well below American levels, they have nevertheless been rising sharply as a multiple of average wages.[6]

Following consultation on the Company Corporate Governance Code, the UK government has accepted several recommendations made by the Business, Energy and Industrial Strategy Select Committee in 2017. Legislation taking effect in 2019 requires listed companies with more than 250 UK employees to produce an annual report outlining what the ratio of CEO pay is to the median pay, to the 25th percentile and to the 75th percentile pay of their UK workforce.[7] And firms also need to produce a narrative explaining reasons for those differences. This development follows the compulsory pay reviews that were put in place to increase the transparency between pay of men and women in big organisations (and are proposed for ethnic pay differences as well). It is possible that any new requirements will be extended to large private firms as well as listed companies.

The Conservative government acknowledges that there are likely to be justifiable differences linked to size of

---

6   Germany's SPD out to cap CEO salaries, *Deutsche Welle*, 24 February 2017 (http://www.dw.com/en/germanys-spd-out-to-cap-ceo-salaries/a-37709 544).

7   Corporate Governance Reform, House of Commons Library, 4 January 2019 (https://researchbriefings.parliament.uk/ResearchBriefing/Summa ry/CBP-8143).

businesses and also to sectors. It recognises that in retail there are large numbers of lower-paid employees in each firm, whereas this isn't the case in the financial sector. There is no suggestion that a cap may be imposed on the private sector: the emphasis is just on publishing and explaining – for the moment, at least. The Labour Party may well go much further if it gets into power.

France on the other hand introduced a cap in 2013, set then at €450k, for executives in the many companies where the state has a majority stake.[8] This was justified on grounds of ethics, justice and transparency and was a multiple of the pay of the lowest 10 per cent of employees in fifteen state companies. The then finance minister, Pierre Moscovici, also promised that salaries in state companies would become public and also expressed hope that the state companies' actions 'would inspire the stabilisation of certain practices in the private sector'. Since then France has also passed a law allowing shareholders a say in the CEO's pay packages and allowing them also to stop each year the performance-related part of the package,[9] following revolt over what were considered to be extravagant compensation awards for the CEOs of Renault and Peugeot, among others. But no actual cap has yet been placed on the pay of executives of private sector companies across the economy.

8   France to cap executive pay at 450,000 euros for state firms, *France 24*, 13 June 2012 (http://www.france24.com/en/20120613-france-moscovici -hollande-ceo-executive-pay-cap-euros-state-firms).

9   French shareholders win say on executive pay, *Financial Times*, 10 June 2016 (https://www.ft.com/content/240318b2-2ed9-11e6-bf8d-26294ad519fc).

Does culture account for some of the differences in attitudes to pay?

Evidence collected by Jelle Bonestroo[10] in 2017 for a thesis for the University of Groningen and Uppsala University suggests that the more individualistic a culture the more necessary it may be to provide strong incentives in the compensation package linked to future growth to ensure that the interests of executives and shareholders are better aligned.

Looking at fourteen countries, the research found that while in the US incentive-based compensation accounted for some 80 per cent of the overall package it represented only 50 per cent of the total package in France and just 27 per cent on average in Japan (Bonestroo 2017). Yet they are all developed economies and members of the G7 with roughly comparable per capita incomes.

How is this possible in an increasingly integrated world economy where top talent can easily move? The answer may lie in different economic structures, varying levels of state involvement in the economy and a more or less dominant financial sector. But is incentive compensation a good thing in itself? Studies suggest that depending on the type of non-salary compensation such packages may in fact offer perverse incentives that encourage too much risk-taking, which, though good for share prices in the short term and providing the CEO with large rewards, may jeopardise the long-term sustainability of a business.

10 CEO incentive-based compensation, investment opportunities and institutional heterogeneity, Uppsala University, 21 March 2017 (http://uu.diva -portal.org/smash/record.jsf?pid=diva2%3A1083291&dswid=7533).

The role of the shareholders here is significant. As we saw when the full drama of the financial crisis unfolded after 2008, in many instances shareholders may have been complicit in supporting excessive short-term risk-taking by managers of companies. The question therefore is whether the current focus of government intervention to enhance shareholder engagement and rights is the correct approach to ensure that directors adhere to long-term performance goals rather than short-term ones. It helps if the company is aware of who its shareholders are. The EU's Shareholder Rights Directive, which came into force in 2017 and is due to start being properly adopted by individual countries in 2019, aims to remedy this by improving the transparency of shareholder arrangements and encouraging greater shareholder involvement in large European companies. It is hoped that, as a consequence, pay will be more reflective of long-term performance than has been the case. The European Commission has also made a number of recommendations on executive pay aimed at tilting the balance away from short-term rewards and also at increasing public perceptions of fairness by suggestions such as banning severance pay in cases of failure (International Finance Corporation 2015).

The directive still gives considerable discretion to individual countries to decide on the exact strength of shareholder rights and on whether votes are binding or not. A number of countries such as the UK have already moved to allow shareholders to vote on remuneration policy. This year the EU will also be able to impose fines for non-implementation of the full directive.[11] Even if the vote ends up being only advisory in some countries, there will still be the requirement that a firm will have to publicly disclose their remuneration policy after a vote and that policy will have to remain on the website for the duration of the period to which it applies. There is no express requirement for firms to abide by a CEO/employee pay ratio. However, a country can transpose into domestic law the need for firms to disclose as a ratio the annual change of each director's pay over a period against the evolution of the average pay of full-time employees, which would increase transparency.

Bonus capping

This is all very welcome for those who seek greater transparency and equity in top pay, particularly as the early focus after the financial crisis seemed just to be on limiting short-term bonuses, at least in Europe. That in itself had some perverse but wholly predictable results. A study in 2014 by Patrick Kampkotter (2015) examined German and Swiss financial sector bonuses before and after the financial crisis, just as the EU cap of paying no more than twice the base salary in the financial sector was being

11 New EU directive to introduce say on pay, govern shareholder intermediaries and establish rules for related party transactions to take effect in 2019, Linklaters, 31 May 2017 (https://www.linklaters.com/en/insights/publications/uk-corporate-update/uk-corporate-update---may-2017/new-eu-directive-to-introduce-say-on-pay-govern-shareholder-intermediaries-and-establish-rules-for-r).

introduced and two years before the regime was tightened further by the European Banking Authority (concerned about the use of extra 'allowances' paid to circumvent the cap) in 2016.[12]

The impact of banks tightening bonuses even before the regulations came into effect was, not surprisingly, a move to higher base salaries, which therefore led to a 'lower performance sensitivity of compensation'. Kampkotter found that fixed compensation packages varied little between banks but there were big differences in bonus payments between individuals. One of the differences between the two countries he studied is that the bonuses compared between companies were broadly similar in Switzerland but seemed to vary greatly between banks in Germany, possibly reflecting widely different fortunes and global reach.

The evidence so far is weak on the question of whether the bonus cap has led to a more secure financial sector. But at least it may have had some impact on assuaging public concern. For the rest of the business sector, that is rather less the case. So while bankers in the EU continue to be subject to bonus cap restrictions, other businesses are not, and the unease continues.

What next?

Despite the important place this issue has taken in the political agenda in many countries, there are problems in

---

12   EU bonus cap: the net widens, PwC, March 2015 (https://www.pwc.com/us/en/industries/financial-services/regulatory-services/library/eu-banker-bonus-cap.html).

tackling it. Looking at practices in OECD nations, the evidence suggests that countries and regions are moving to greater transparency and there are increasing voluntary and regulatory requirements for organisations to justify the pay they award their top executives. The financial sector has been under greater scrutiny but large chunks of business outside the banking system – for example, hedge funds and non-listed financial intermediaries – still seem very much to do their own thing without any constraints.

Very high rewards still seem to be there across most sectors, for example in business services (such as the rewards of the former CEO of WPP, Martin Sorrell,[13] until his recent departure), in earnings of founders and directors of the large tech firms (Facebook, for example) which are now coming under increasing scrutiny given the mounting concerns over perceived dubious practices and misuse of data. And there are concerns about compensation in firms which are argued to be making inadequate payments to the tax authorities despite high turnover volumes in many countries (Google and Amazon in the UK). Yet many firms proudly display their corporate and social responsibility reports while keeping executive pay at a huge multiple of median wages in their firms.

A 2016 PwC study using Pew Research Centre and OECD data[14] found widespread concern about inequality among OECD countries, though surprisingly countries such as

---

13 WPP's Sir Martin Sorrell turned a tiny firm into a global titan, BBC News, 15 April 2018 (https://www.bbc.co.uk/news/business-43668207).

14 Time to listen, PwC, 1 July 2016 (https://www.pwc.co.uk/services/human -resource-services/insights/time-to-listen.html).

Italy, France and Spain worried about it a lot more than people in the UK and the US, where inequality is much greater.[15] Nevertheless, research carried out by Opinium for PwC found that even in the UK some two thirds of the population believed that top pay was too high and 87 per cent believed that the issue needed to be addressed. And there was a widespread view that pay should be limited to no more than twenty times average earnings.

The problem is that individual countries will hesitate to do much more until they can see clearly the evidence that caps or other measures will eventually lead to an improvement in company performance and that from the economy's perspective these measures actually result in a better allocation of resources.

In theory anything that links performance to the long-term sustainability of a company should be good for growth and productivity. The measures so far seem to have tackled perverse short-term incentives but it remains to be seen whether they end up really incentivising longer-term growth. Share buybacks and lack of investment in productive capacity still seem to be common. Critics of high pay argue that more needs to be done in an internationally coordinated manner to achieve fundamental change in incentives and to improve the perceived fairness of rewards.

---

15 Interestingly, the issue of 'fairness' in relation to executive pay was correlated less with actual inequality in a country but more to concerns and anxiety about jobs and stagnating wage growth.

6 TWO KINDS OF TOP PAY

Paul Ormerod[1]

Introduction

The dramatic rise in the remuneration of top earners relative to most of the labour force is well documented. Forty years ago, the typical compensation of a CEO in America was around thirty times greater than that of the average employee. By the mid 1990s, this ratio had risen to 100 to 1, and now it is over 300 times as much. In the UK, to give a smaller-scale example, there is much controversy over the way in which the salaries of university vice-chancellors – university presidents in America – have grown enormously, even in the most undistinguished institutions.

These developments have attracted a great deal of adverse comment in the media. Popular resentment is high. Yet the even greater amounts of money made by both entrepreneurs and stars of popular culture appear to be accepted with equanimity.

For example, in 2018 (according to *Forbes*), George Clooney earned $239 million and Dwayne Johnson was the

---

1 I am very grateful to an anonymous referee for some stimulating and helpful comments.

second highest among male actors at $119 million.[2] The same magazine noted that, in the year to June 2018, the 100 best-paid athletes made $3.8 billion between them.[3] The boxer Floyd Mayweather topped the list with $285 million. Even these sums are of course dwarfed by the wealth of entrepreneurs such as Mark Zuckerberg and the late Steve Jobs.

The public's apparent unconcern about some people's fabulous incomes may seem paradoxical. However, I will argue shortly that economic theory offers a sound justification for these stupendous numbers in popular culture and in entrepreneurship.

By contrast the rewards of corporate board members are harder to justify, though there is an extensive literature in economics which attempts to do precisely that. It might be thought that this is a challenging task. Until relatively recently in the corporate world, to become seriously rich you had to be an entrepreneur and take risks with your own money. What we have seen with the rise in CEO remuneration is that mere employees who are only risking other people's money, not their own, have also been able to become seriously rich.[4]

---

2 The world's highest-paid actors 2018: George Clooney tops the list with $239 million, *Forbes*, 22 August 2018 (https://www.forbes.com/sites/nata lierobehmed/2018/08/22/the-worlds-highest-paid-actors-2018-george -clooney-tops-list-with-239-million/#7154e5e17dfd).

3 Full list: the world's highest-paid athletes 2018, *Forbes*, 13 June 2018 (https://www.forbes.com/sites/kurtbadenhausen/2018/06/13/full-list-the -worlds-highest-paid-athletes-2018/#915d89f7d9f9).

4 This applies to a wider range of employees in the banking and financial sectors, though I do not discuss them here.

In this chapter I consider arguments made by some leading economists in defence of corporate top pay levels. I also offer a broad perspective on the empirical evidence. But a distinguishing feature of my analysis is to make a case that the rise in corporate pay can be accounted for by the spread of social norms.

Top pay in popular culture

The top-ranked *Journal of Economic Perspectives* had a symposium of papers in one of its 2013 issues on the 'top one per cent'. The paper by the leading Harvard economist Greg Mankiw was explicitly entitled 'Defending the one per cent'.

Mankiw relies essentially on two arguments, both of which are based upon technology. He cites with approval the work of Goldin and Katz (2008), who argue that technological change usually increases the demand for skilled labour. Unless society is able to educate and train people so that the supply of skilled labour increases at least as much as the demand, the earnings of skilled workers will rise relative to the rest of the labour force. As Mankiw (2013: 23) puts it, 'the story of rising inequality there is not primarily about rent seeking, but rather about supply and demand'.

We might wonder what the impact of the huge growth in business schools in recent decades has been. These are meant to teach executive skills and so the supply of people capable of filling top executive roles might be presumed to have increased substantially.

Mankiw does concede that the Goldin and Katz arguments apply to the broad changes in inequality in general, and are not necessarily focused on the rewards of the top 1 per cent. But Mankiw invokes a further aspect of technology to account for why pay at the very top has grown so spectacularly.

Changes in technology have allowed a small number of often highly educated and exceptionally talented individuals to command superstar incomes in a way which was not possible a generation ago. Brynjolfsson and McAfee argue this strongly in their book *Race Against the Machine*. Mankiw quotes from the book: 'aided by digital technologies, entrepreneurs, entertainment stars and financial executives have been able to leverage their talents across global markets and capture reward that would have been unimaginable in earlier times' (Brynjolfsson and McAfee 2011: 44).

A similar argument was used well before the digital revolution really took off, by Sherwin Rosen (1981) in his paper 'The economics of superstars'. This is the article invoked by Kaplan and Rauh (2013), also defending the pay of the top 1 per cent, in the same issue of the *Journal of Economic Perspectives* as the Mankiw article.

An example which Rosen gave very early on in his paper was 'sales of elementary textbooks in economics are concentrated on a group of best sellers, though there exist a large number of very good and highly substitutable alternatives in the market' (Rosen 1981: 845). This shows an amusing prescience, given that Mankiw is the author of what is perhaps the number one basic textbook of our times.

Rosen's arguments are based on some subtle concepts in economic theory, and the paper itself rapidly becomes rather dense in its use of maths for the general reader. Even when set out in English, they require some effort to follow.

The key is what is described in the jargon of economics as a 'public good'. It is important to realise that the phrase is not being used here in any natural sense. It has a specific, technical meaning in economics.

A classic example of a public good in economics is defence. Individuals cannot effectively be excluded from consuming it, and the use of it by one person does not reduce the availability of it to others. To introduce some more jargon, a public good is 'non-excludable' and 'non-rival in consumption'.

So, for example, once a decision has been made to provide a country with a nuclear deterrent, no citizen can be excluded from the services which it provides. Indeed, in this case even the most ardent pacifist is obliged to 'consume' it. And the fact that one individual benefits from its existence does not mean that anyone else is prevented from benefiting to the same extent. If I buy up all the bananas on a market stall, until the seller restocks the stall, no one else can buy them. But this is not the case with a public good.

In essence, public goods are not consumed individually, but jointly.

Even in the pre-internet era, radio, television and the telephone had greatly increased the level of connectivity in society. A hundred years ago, for example, the only people who could have any direct experience of Manchester United playing soccer live were those present in the stadium during the game. In 1927, the BBC began broadcasting live football commentary on radio. Although the BBC[5] began transmitting soccer on television in 1938, the games were few and far between, and regular coverage did not start until the early 1960s. It was only around that time that more than 50 per cent of UK households had a TV. Now, of course, Manchester United can be watched by literally billions around the world, using a variety of delivery channels.

Rosen argued that the provision of many cultural services, for example (and using the word 'culture' in a wide sense) involves joint consumption, not unlike a public good. A performer or author must make the same effort almost regardless of whether 100 or 100,000 people watch him or her, or read the book. The costs of production do not really rise with the size of the market.

However, the difference between this technology and a public good is that people can be, and are, excluded from consumption. Unless you pay, you don't get to see the show or read the book. But the joint consumption features of these products and services means that a relatively small number of sellers can in principle service the entire market. And the more talented they are, the fewer still are needed.

So, as Rosen (1981: 847) puts it, 'the possibility for talented persons to command both very large markets and very large incomes is apparent'.

Kaplan and Rauh argue that, in the age of the internet, the arguments made by Rosen have become even more powerful. Professional athletes and artists, for example, can now reach much bigger markets than ever before.

---

5   Which then held a domestic monopoly on radio and television in the UK.

Technology enables Wall Street investors and executives to acquire information and trade in hitherto unimaginable amounts.

There is considerable validity in the opinions offered by Mankiw and (via Rosen) Kaplan and Rauh. But these arguments are much more relevant to stars of popular culture and to entrepreneurs than they are to the board members of massive companies which have been around for a considerable amount of time.

As far as entrepreneurs are concerned, we can also invoke the argument made by Schumpeter (1934). A successful innovation, which provides a product or service which did not previously exist, enables the entrepreneur to earn monopoly profits until such time as competitors are able either to replicate the innovation or to produce a superior competitor.

The theoretical justifications for the earnings of pop stars, actors, athletes and entrepreneurs appear to be well founded. In practice, people do not seem to begrudge these individuals their rewards, vast though they may be. They are perceived as being based upon individual merit.

Top pay and corporate executives

In the simple models of basic economics textbooks, individuals are rewarded in line with their productivity. The more value they add to the organisation, the more they get paid.

In the jargon of economics, this is known as marginal revenue productivity theory. In competitive conditions, it is asserted, employees will receive the value of their marginal contribution to a firm's revenue. Straightforward expositions of this proposition are readily available on the internet, so there is no need to expound the argument in detail here.

Marginal contributions may be fairly easy to see on factory production lines, in restaurants or in fruit picking. When we are considering the pay of, say, CEOs, the theory is more complicated. It reflects an important discussion in economics which dates back to the end of the nineteenth century, and is still very much alive today.

In the decades before World War I, two highly accomplished mathematicians who occupied the top chairs in economics at the time, Alfred Marshall at Cambridge and Francis Edgeworth at Oxford, wrangled over the issue.

Edgeworth thought that, in most situations, there was an inherent indeterminacy about the price which emerged – in the current context the 'price' is the salary of the CEO. He wrote: 'It may be said that in pure economics there is only one theorem, but that it is a very difficult one: the theory of bargain'.[6]

Marshall simplified matters dramatically. He assumed there are so many economic agents in a market that no single one of them can influence the price. This enabled him to draw, in his own best-selling textbook, the supply and demand curve diagrams familiar to generations of students.

---

6   F. Y. Edgeworth, 'On the application of mathematics to political economy', reproduced in Marchionatti (2004: 137).

At the time, Marshall prevailed. His textbook dominated the teaching of economics for decades. Recently, Edgeworth has returned with a vengeance. A lot of modern economic theory is about developing Edgeworth's view that economics is basically about bargaining. It makes theory much more difficult, but potentially more realistic.

The implication is that there may be a wide range of possible outcomes to any given bargaining process, rather than there being a unique one dictated by marginal productivity theory.

Nevertheless, the idea that executive contracts somehow represent an optimal outcome retains a strong following in economics.

A recent and very detailed survey of the literature on executive pay was carried out by Edmans et al. (2017). They spend considerable time discussing what they call the 'shareholder value' view of CEO pay. This proposes that CEO contracts are the outcome of shareholder value-maximising firms competing in an efficient market for managerial talent.

The authors immediately qualify the concept of optimality in this context. For example, the optimal contract theoretically may be highly non-linear and never be observed in reality. More generally, they describe what they term 'bounded rationality' where boards are not aware of some performance measures that 'could theoretically improve the contract if included'.

A reasonable interpretation of the latter phrase is that it describes imperfect information rather than bounded rationality in the sense which Nobel Laureate Herbert Simon used the phrase. Simon (1955) believed that in most practical situations it is simply not possible to know the optimal strategy to follow or the optimal decision to make. It is not a matter of a simple lack of information. The environment in which agents take decisions is too complex at a point in time and it evolves in too unpredictable a manner over time, for the concept of optimality to have any meaning.

Nevertheless, even though optimality may not be a terribly useful concept in this context, it is of course still possible that the main motivation in determining executive contracts is an attempt to increase shareholder value.

Edmans and his colleagues suggest that there are three main hypotheses put forward in the literature to account for the huge increase in executive pay in recent decades.

The first is the 'shareholder value' one already mentioned. The second is the 'rent extraction' view, which argues that contracts are set by executives themselves to maximise their own rents. The final perspective is that pay is shaped by institutional forces, such as regulation, tax and accounting policies.

The conclusion which is drawn is firm, while at the same time being heavily guarded. From an empirical perspective, the authors argue that no single hypothesis can explain all the evidence. The outcomes which are observed are some combination of all three.

They also emphasise further limitations to our ability to draw unequivocal conclusions. For example, much of the formal theory around the issue has been developed for the 'shareholder value' approach. But they point out that seemingly innocuous differences in assumptions in models can lead to quite different outcomes. Further, this hypothesis is consistent with a wide range of potential empirical outcomes.

Much of the evidence discussed in the paper is, however, of a detailed and technical nature. In the next section, I set the discussion around executive pay in a broader context.

A broad perspective on the empirical evidence

We might usefully begin with a thought experiment. Imagine someone working for, say, $10 an hour. We wave a wand, and are in a world where everything else remains unchanged but the same worker is now paid just $5 an hour. We could reasonably expect an adverse impact on this person's motivation.

Now consider someone receiving $10.1 million a year, which according to Edmans and colleagues was the median CEO compensation in the S&P 500 companies in 2014. Our wand performs the same trick, and this is reduced to $5.05 million. It requires more imagination to believe that someone paid this amount would somehow be insufficiently motivated to perform his or her job.

The fact is that, for long periods of time, CEOs and other top executives were paid very considerably less than they are now, and the economy nevertheless performed well.

Edmans and colleagues cite calculations by Frydman and Saks (2010) on the real levels of compensation of the three highest paid executives in the fifty largest US companies since the late 1930s. From the end of World War II to around 1970, the median level of total compensation was just under $2 million a year in 2014 dollars. It is now well in excess of $10 million.

It may of course be important to an individual company that Mrs Smith rather than Mr Jones is appointed as CEO, and the markets can and do take an interest in such things. But the relevant context is not that of the individual company, but of the corporate sector as a whole, and within this the large companies which dominate the economy.

Given the increase in CEO compensation, we would expect to see an improved performance of the overall economy in recent decades. The evidence, however, points firmly in the opposite direction. The rate of growth of the economy as a whole has slowed. Real GDP in the US grew by 3.5 per cent a year between 1957 and 1987, but by only 2.5 per cent between 1987 and 2017.

GDP of course measures the output of the economy, the amount of goods and services which are produced. The value of companies is more complex, and is not simply related to how fast their revenues are growing. It depends upon the expected future stream of dividends which investors might receive in return for holding equities.

Strong revenue growth might well increase the value of a company. But investors will look not just at the actual profits which are made on those revenues – because dividends can only be paid from profits – but will also form expectations about the future growth in profits.

Undoubtedly, the market value of major companies has grown spectacularly in recent decades. Stock markets across the West have boomed, the crash of the late 2000s notwithstanding. In 1987, the Dow Jones stood at – using very round numbers here to make comparisons easy – about 2,000. In 2017 it averaged some 22,000: an eleven-fold increase, which represents a dramatic acceleration of growth compared with the three decades immediately preceding, from 1957 to 1987. Over this earlier period, the Dow Jones rose from 500 to 2,000.

The contrast is even more marked when we examine the average annual rate of growth in real terms, after allowing for inflation. Between 1957 and 1987, the Dow Jones rose by 4.6 per cent a year, but inflation averaged 4.3 per cent. Effectively, it was more or less unchanged in real terms. For the period 1987–2017, the comparable numbers are 8.3 per cent and 2.1 per cent, a real increase of over 6 per cent a year.

Valuing financial assets is of course a complex business. The American economist Robert Shiller got the Nobel Prize for his analysis of financial markets. Using over a century's worth of data, he showed that the short-term fluctuations in share prices were much greater than those of the dividend streams which were paid out.[7]

But over longer periods, certainly over several decades, the excess swings in equity prices, both up and down, should to a substantial extent cancel each other out. We should expect to see over the longer run a closer, albeit still not perfect, relationship between changes in the stock market and changes in the prospect of firms' earnings.

The rate at which output is expanding has slowed in recent decades, so we might imagine that the growth in

---

7   Robert J. Shiller Prize Lecture, The Nobel Prize, 8 December 2013 (https://www.nobelprize.org/prizes/economics/2013/shiller/lecture/).

the earnings of companies had also slowed. However, the amount of profit which companies make from any given level of output has risen.

The share of wages in national income was essentially the same in the late 1980s as it was in the late 1950s. But since then, there has been a fall of some four percentage points, and a similar rise in the profit share.[8] This may seem small, but in money terms it amounts to almost $1 trillion a year.

The rise in asset prices – and hence the value of companies – is underpinned by the fact that profits have grown faster than the economy as a whole over the past three decades.

Might this, then, be a rational explanation for the boom in top executive pay? The stock market value of companies has also boomed, and executive remuneration has risen commensurately.

This explanation is, however, rather undermined by a detailed analysis of CEO pay at the individual firm level carried out by Ethan Rouen of Harvard Business School. Rouen (2017) obtained confidential establishment-level annual data provided by the US Bureau of Labor Statistics for a large sample of firms in the S&P 1,500 from 2006 to 2013. He found 'no statistically significant relation between the ratio of CEO-to-mean employee compensation and performance'. In other words, in publicly traded companies there was no

---

8   In the national economic accounts, there are some minor categories of income other than wages and profits, so that changes in the two are not exactly equal and opposite.

connection between how much the CEO was paid relative to the average worker and how well the company did.

More generally, there has been a very powerful factor operating across the developed world over the past three decades or so which has held wages down relative to profits. The absorption of China and India into the global economy from around 1990 onwards added over a billion workers to world labour supply. This process created downward pressure on wage rates, particularly among the less skilled.

Less dramatically, many of the countries in Eastern Europe which were under Soviet domination entered into the capitalist world after the fall of the Berlin Wall in 1989. Christian Dustmann of University College London and colleagues provide detailed evidence on the impact on wages in the old West Germany of the opening up of economies such as Poland and the Czech Republic.

The implication of their empirical evidence is that CEOs *in general* have not created the massive rise in stock markets, and therefore the value of companies, by their skill and enterprise. They appear to have simply ridden on the backs of the powerful economic forces which generated the growth in the profitability of companies (Dustmann et al. 2014).

A network perspective

Earlier we argued that many prices – and executive compensation is one such price – are set not at a unique level determined by supply and demand, but by a process of bargaining. There is a potentially wide range of indeterminacy in the price which emerges from any process of bargaining.

The existing literature within economics on executive pay largely neglects the role of social norms, and how these may evolve and influence the bargaining process.

One of the most rapidly growing areas of knowledge in the past two decades or so has been the field of networks, more specifically, knowledge about how ideas, beliefs, behaviours and the like either spread or are contained in networks of connected agents.

The phrase 'connected agents' means agents who are connected to each other in the sense that one, or both, of them has the potential to influence the behaviour of the other in a specific context. The group of others who may influence any given agent may, indeed almost certainly will, vary from setting to setting. I may, for example, pay attention to the opinions of certain people on restaurants, but when it comes to thinking about financial products, I look to an entirely different set of people.

Two key assumptions of standard economic theory are that the tastes and preferences of each 'agent' (individual or business entity) are both formed independently and do not vary over time. The decisions that an agent takes can certainly be affected by what others do, but only indirectly via prices. I may like bananas and go to the market intending to buy some, only to find that demand has been high today and the price has gone up so much that I choose not to buy any. But my liking for bananas has not altered. If the price is lower tomorrow, I will buy.

In a networked world of the type discussed here, these assumptions no longer hold. A seminal paper, many years ahead of its time, was by Nobel Laureate Thomas Schelling (1973). With the intriguing title 'Hockey helmets, concealed weapons and daylight-saving time', Schelling was inspired by a story in the sports pages of his local newspaper.

An ice hockey player had not been wearing a helmet and had suffered serious head injuries when struck by the puck. The rational choice was to wear a helmet. When a star player was asked why he continued not to wear one, he replied 'I don't because the other guys don't'. In other words, his preferences were not fixed. They were determined by the behaviour of others.

Twenty years later, the now famous paper by Bikhchandani and colleagues (1992) described how information cascades can grow through 'rational herding' in a sequential social learning process, with each agent balancing what he or she already knows against what others can be seen to be doing.

A landmark paper on how behaviours and opinions spread across networks was published by the mathematical sociologist Duncan Watts. In this model (Watts 2002), agents pay no attention at all to the attributes of the alternatives presented to them, in complete contrast to standard economic theory. Their decisions are based entirely on what the agents to which they are connected – those which can potentially influence them – do.

A key point from both the Bikhchandani et al. paper and the much more formal analysis by Watts is that the information which spreads, the ideas which become popular, are not necessarily those which have superior qualities to the rest.

Indeed, in the Watts paper by definition no single alternative is better than any of the others. Agents can only be in one of two 'states of the world'. To give a contemporary UK example, an agent could either want to remain in the EU or be in favour of leaving. By construction in Watts's model, at the start all agents hold the same view. Then a few, at random, change their mind. Agents base their decisions solely on the opinions of those to which they are connected.

Most of the time, the switch of opinion fizzles out. But occasionally, there is a 'global cascade' across the network, and almost all agents alter their initial opinion. In essence, the eventual size of the change depends upon some rather subtle mathematical properties of the structure of the network.

Of course, in practice things are much more complex. Scientific models such as those of Bikhchandani and Watts make deliberate simplifications in order to get a better understanding of reality.

The key point to draw from this is that the optimal choice among the alternatives in any given situation does not necessarily win out. This goes against the arguments put forward by, for example, Mankiw. He implicitly assumes that the market always leads to optimal outcomes. Modern technology simply enables rewards to a small number of talented individuals to be leveraged on a massive scale.

There could be justification for the size of the reward if the best really did emerge. In sport, for example, it is usually pretty clear. Either Bolt runs faster than you or he does not. It is much less clear cut among CEOs as to who is actually the best.

What executives *have* been really good at is in ensuring that the narrative that they in some way deserve their pay has become the dominant one in the relevant network. The network here is the pool of people from whom non-executive directors, management consultants with the large firms, remuneration 'experts' and the like are drawn.

Before the financial crisis, Piketty and Saez (2006: 204) advanced the argument that executive pay had grown so rapidly because of 'the increased ability of executives to set their own pay and extract rents at the expense of shareholders'. They did not suggest exactly how this had happened. But the view is consistent with the idea that a set of values which had previously held top pay in check has been replaced, in the relevant network, by a set in which traditional constraints no longer obtain.

Conclusion

Although the arguments of this chapter have perhaps been complex, the conclusion to be drawn can be stated rather simply.

The dramatic rise in the remuneration of athletes, film stars, musicians and entrepreneurs has a sound justification in economic theory. It has been created by the huge advances in technology, principally communications technology in the broader sense.

The increase in executive pay, in contrast, is hard to justify, whether from a theoretical or from an empirical perspective. In my view, it is difficult to escape the conclusion that it has been primarily based on successful rent-seeking.

7   TOP PAY FOR WOMEN

Judy Z. Stephenson and Sophie Jarvis

Introduction

There is a gender pay gap at all earnings levels. The relatively few women at the top of large organisations such as FTSE-100 companies can earn substantial amounts of money, but even they earn much less than their male counterparts.[1] However, it is not at all clear that the underlying cause of this pay gap is unfair discrimination. The results of the UK's new compulsory gender pay reporting by large organisations tell us what we already knew, that pay *is* gendered, but they also show that the reasons for this are complex. In this chapter we try to explain how labour markets work, and how they work for different groups, as a means of understanding what can or should be done to ameliorate labour market gender inequality

It is tempting to write a chapter that champions the cause of women's pay and equality as a matter of government policy, labour law and equal rights. To do so would be timely and probably quite popular, though rather

---

1   Pay gap: what seven women FTSE CEOs earned in 2017, *Wealth Manager*, 15 August 2018 (https://citywire.co.uk/wealth-manager/news/pay-gap -what-seven-women-ftse-ceos-earned-in-2017/a1146884).

predictable. But there is a more interesting, and useful, discussion about women and their pay to be had – why are there a small number of women earning top pay in some sectors rather than others?

Gender pay gap basics

First, some basics. According to a recent YouGov survey,[2] 64 per cent of people erroneously believe that the gender pay gap means paying men and women different amounts for the same work, i.e. unequal pay. Much of the heated debate around the gender pay gap has been caused by this confusion. The gender pay gap is in fact defined as a measure of the difference between men's and women's average[3] earnings in an organisation or the labour market as a whole. It is expressed as a percentage of men's earnings. The gender pay gap for hourly pay across the UK in 2018 was 9.1 per cent for full-time workers. The gap is largely attributable to different kinds of careers and working patterns. Generally, men work in higher-paid occupations, and they are more likely to work full time in those higher-paid occupations. They have longer career trajectories, and steadier work. While the reasons for these are the outcome of many social, educational and possibly discriminatory inequalities

---

2   Most Brits have the wrong idea of what the gender pay gap is, YouGov, 14 September 2018 (https://yougov.co.uk/topics/economy/articles/repor ts/2018/09/14/most-brits-have-wrong-idea-what-gender-pay-gap).

3   This can be the *mean* or the *median*: the gap is greater for mean earnings, but the Office for National Statistics prefers the median measure as it is more representative of 'typical' experience.

and gendered patterns, it is rare that men and women are paid different amounts for identical work, which would be illegal. The gender pay gap is much more complex.[4]

As statistical analysis of the reported figures by the ONS[5] shows, only just over a third of the difference in gendered pay for all workers (36.1 per cent) can be explained by factors that affect labour market earnings generally – age, sector, tenure, working pattern, business size and region. Occupation (men are attracted to and generally work in higher-paying occupations, while some occupations that are seen as traditionally male pay more) accounts for almost a quarter of the difference between men and women's pay. The second biggest explanatory factor is working patterns. Women earn roughly the same as men in most occupations until childbearing age or motherhood. Women are much more likely to work in part-time roles, and in part-time work they earn more than male part-timers – but in the long run part-time roles pay less well, because part-time workers do not attain the same seniority in large organisations as full-time ones. Although tenure is a huge determinant of pay in the labour market generally – men and women who have worked for one employer for more than twenty years earn on average 20 per cent more than

4 So too is the ethnic pay gap, which is coming under increased scrutiny. Many of the arguments about the reasons for pay inequality discussed in this chapter apply to ethnic disadvantage as well.

5 See: Understanding the gender pay gap in the UK, Office for National Statistics, 17 January 2018 (https://www.ons.gov.uk/employmentandlabour market/peopleinwork/earningsandworkinghours/articles/understandi ngthegenderpaygapintheuk/2018-01-17#a-breakdown-of-the-gender-pay -gap).

people who have worked for an employer for one year – the effect is very similar for both men and women and so it accounts for only just over 2 per cent of the difference between them.

The unaccounted-for gender pay gap

This still leaves the largest part – almost two thirds of the considerable gap between what men and women earn in the labour market – as 'unexplained'. There is a common belief that the gender pay gap is related to sexual discrimination. Pay inequality may be related to sexual discrimination, but it is not directly caused by it. Employers who respect the law don't generally set out to pay women less. Women are thought to be less confident in asking for pay rises – but does this explain such a significant chunk?

We are taught to understand labour markets as markets where, in simplified terms, labour and skill are exchanged for wages and the position of a job. Associated with this is the idea that wages should be 'fair' and that more productive workers will be paid more. Key to the idea of wage equality is that similar levels of skill should be rewarded similarly. But labour markets are not exchanges for skill and wages – they are markets where *information* is exchanged and where skill only plays a small part in determining pay.

Workers seek information about the availability of work, wages, hours, colleagues, commutes and various working conditions, while employers seek information about the availability of workers, their likely cost and productivity, and their personal characteristics. The information that both sides have is imperfect and asymmetric in that neither side can ever truly obtain the information they seek about the other, but in the attempt or completion of every transaction many different types of information are gathered.

By way of example, an employer in Exeter who hires a 35-year-old male accountant, with a degree in management from the University of Nottingham, six years of post-CIMA experience and a wife and two children, living in Tiverton, on a permanent, four-day-a-week contract and finds he does the work required very well and is faster at producing the quarterly updates than his predecessor might be predisposed to other Nottingham graduates, other management graduates, other 35-year-old males, other people from Tiverton with a wife and two children, other CIMA-qualified accountants or all of the above. A warehouse manager who hires two Polish women to count stock part-time through an agency and finds them to be efficient, tidier and more accurate than the English school leavers who were doing the job until last week has gathered information about the agency, Polish female stock checkers, the youths she was using until last week, and how quickly she can fill such a position. A major retailer who poaches a marketing executive from a rival gathers information about the rival's marketing plans and wage rates as well as the kind of information on personal performance and characteristics described above.

It is clear that gender is part of the personal characteristics of any employer or employee, and the associations about how one's gender may affect work is what equality legislation tries to regulate. It's also clear from the descriptions above that personal circumstances and choices about working conditions will affect work choice. The 35-year-old accountant might not have been keen on a commute to Bristol because he drops his three-year-old at nursery on the way to work, and he simply was not available five days a week. This is more difficult to legislate for. Society does not legislate the division of labour inside the home (although there are some who believe that we should do more in that regard). We know that women are still doing two-thirds of all housework and domestic chores, and this and parenting responsibilities are usually given as the explanation for why they choose part-time work.

The information gap

Because the performance of any employee (or the working conditions at any employer) cannot be known before work begins, the information that is exchanged in the labour market is exchanged outside of employment or in what we might call the 'open market' where potential employers and employees transact through signalling. Qualifications, previous employment history and other personal characteristics indicate to employers that employees will be productive. Share prices, media and marketing, the quality of the coffee and the office furniture, the style of any uniform and premises all signal to employees what working conditions might be. Employers and employees use such signals to sort potential matches and the business of exchanging this information is what we all recognise as job search.

Information is also exchanged *internally,* within firms, as performance becomes known. Changes to working conditions such as hours, benefits and team changes also give both sides information about relative performance and likely future behaviour. If the employer of accountants in Exeter described above had never previously employed an accountant on a four-day-week contract, they will have gathered information on part-time workers through the performance of the 35-year-old male. But the 35-year-old male will be missing information on what happens in the office on the fifth day.

Part-time work

There is a large volume of research showing that, particularly in the professions and more skilled occupations, women suffer a 'career penalty' for motherhood. Generally, the pattern is that women participate equally in the labour force until they have children, then leave for a time – either for maternity leave or for extended parental leave, or out of the labour force altogether for a period – and when they return they don't see the same progression. Although it is not entirely clear from the figures, it is true that mothers are more likely to work part time, and part-time workers are less likely to rise to senior positions in organisations. This may be because those who choose to work part-time miss out on key information and networking opportunities that advance a worker's career. Similarly, employers may not invest in them through training as much as full-time employees. It seems fair to many people that those who stay late and are always available and reliable are the ones who receive top pay, not those who are trying to do something else important as well as the job. Although this might sound harsh, in reality there is no difference to a firm whether their employees, outside of working hours, are looking after their child or enjoying extra leisure time. As women predominantly take more part-time work than men, rewards to those who spend more time at the office hit them hardest. In the long run this means women on average don't receive top pay, and are sidelined into work that pays less.

The 'ratchet effect' and the gender pay gap

Research into markets for information broadly predicts two things that are relevant to gendered pay. The first is that in any market for information there is always some dispersion in the price paid for a good – or in this case the wages paid for a particular level of skill – because information is *always* imperfect. What this means is that the same product will be offered at different prices from different sellers because they will each add different services or benefits or costs to the product. Different negotiations with different people produce slightly different outcomes. Prices tend to converge when there are lots of transactions – meaning lots of information – or where there is little information (or skill) required. In markets where there is a lot of activity, information eventually travels well and everyone understands the 'going rate' or usual price. In markets where there aren't many transactions, information may be hard to find, and search costs very considerable. This means that absolute equality of pay or reward for everyone doing the same work is uncommon, but it is more likely at the lower-skilled end of the market or where there is a high turnover of staff. Employers find out that they are not paying enough when lots of people quit. Sometimes employers 'wage post' at a slightly premium wage to attract and retain workers and avoid the costs of hiring and having to gather so much information. For women workers what this means is that gender inequality in pay is likely to be least in lower-skilled occupations, and where there are lots of transactions, or where there are lots of transactions by both men and women.

For example, take the accountancy profession. A qualified accountant in the UK has broadly the same qualification as all the other 260,000 accountants in the country. By contrast, there is no standardised qualification for TV presenters and broadcasters. And there are nowhere near 260,000 TV presenters and broadcasters in the UK. Women working in accounting are more likely to be paid fairly as there is plenty of information and there are plenty of ways to signal in this market. In the TV industry there are fewer signals and fewer players.

Another comparison would be the housing market. It's very easy to discern the 'right' price of a house on a street where there are twenty other houses that all look fairly similar. It's a lot harder to discern the price of a remote house, where there are significantly fewer comparisons.

Limited information and less time spent in the workplace makes women more susceptible to inequality in one important aspect of workplace and pay bargaining – the 'ratchet effect'. The ratchet effect relates to situations where workers who are paid for their performance – or paid 'fairly' – face a bargain with employers over the way that this performance is assessed. If workers give a very high output or level of productivity, they fear – often correctly – that employers will change the way they assess performance, to set the bar higher or 'move the goalposts'. The ratchet is the upward movement of productivity or effort expectation. Workers respond by limiting output or effort short of their absolute highest level of productivity. Employers respond by sanctioning certain behaviours – breaks, holiday timings and duration, expenses and so on. Such bargaining is subtle, strategic and ongoing in all aspects of workplace activity. Women who feel less secure in their positions because they have other dependencies – childcare or elder care, a need for flexible hours – will limit output less, and may in fact give more to try to gain security. If they spend less time in the workplace they don't see and absorb the 'rules of the game' that everyone else is observing about output and productivity. Co-workers who are more regular may sense this and exclude them from networks. This can directly impact on their career progression. In other words, women may be at a disadvantage in the subtle game of pay bargaining inherent in workplace behaviours and performance standards.

Networking gap

Which leads on to another issue: people with better net-works and information do better or gain more in such markets. Search costs in labour markets are the costs of finding and retrieving information about two things. Firstly, workers don't know if the kind of work they would like to do, in the kinds of organisations they would like, at the kind of pay rate they would like is available until they begin to search for work. This kind of information is market information – is there a going rate? What is the usual contract and terms? Secondly, they don't really know what the job will entail and whether the hours, co-workers, culture, expectations and other aspects of jobs that people find important will suit them. This kind of information is organisation-specific, and in any career progression commonly happens in the organisation's *internal* labour market. Some labour market information can only be gathered by working for a particular kind of employer. This explains the clubbiness that people who have worked for secretive or idiosyncratic organisations can display.

If there are few women, or people that she knows, in the sector, occupation or firm that a woman would like to work in, then information will be harder to come by and she is at greater risk of getting a poor deal. Firstly, search is potentially more difficult for women. In order to gather information about what working at a firm at a given pay rate will be like for them, they need to find others like them, and in the best-paid professions there are fewer women to glean information from. The market is thin. In thin markets it is harder to search, and transactions are harder to put together. One can illustrate the concept by showing how search becomes more difficult later in women's careers. A young woman who is searching for her first job after university has information from all her peers and from university careers services and employers who advertise. Her information is probably as good as any of her friends', whether male or female. Fifteen years later, after maternity leave, and extended parental leave to help look after children, and working in a part-time role, she is much more isolated. There are fewer like her in her chosen occupation, and because they are part time they see each other and possibly exchange information less.

Almost counterintuitively, this means that women in very specialist or very idiosyncratic work may have very high or very low pay – but because it's much harder to know what the pay 'should' be, it will all come down to individual bargaining, rather than signalling and information. This explains why some women in specialised fields – such as the well-publicised BBC cases – have very good outcomes, and some very bad. It's much harder to say what is 'fair' if there is no market information. Some BBC women were indeed being paid different amounts for doing the same job and having more or less the same experience. The one case that dominated the news, Carrie Gracie,[6] was a situation where there were very few comparable signals to offer information to either side, yet the reportage treated this as a

6   BBC reaches equal pay deal with former China editor Carrie Gracie, *The Guardian*, 29 June 2018 (https://www.theguardian.com/media/2018/jun/29/bbc-reach-equal-pay-deal-with-former-china-editor-carrie-gracie).

straightforward story of inequality. To say this should not exonerate the BBC, and many similar organisations, for some very poor monitoring of performance and general HR standards. It is to highlight that unless we understand how such pay bargains happen, and how pay information works in the labour market, the inequalities that many people understand as 'discrimination' will persist.

Better information

What does this all mean for the gender pay gap? If the labour market is one for information, then good information – real data on what matters and how markets work – is vital for women. So the information being gathered from the compulsory reporting of all organisations with over 250 employees is very good news for women – and men – because it gives everyone better information. Everyone can search for information on pay gaps in their firms, in their sectors and in their occupations. The fact that the information is available to everyone also has a positive impact if misinformation is a reason behind the pay gap. The real news is that the reasons for the differences in men's and women's pay are multifarious and the outcome of many choices, behaviours and signals. Labelling the gender pay gap as about discrimination risks 'informing' women that they are all victims of injustice. This is poor information. This would not do young women (or young men) any favours in the workplace in terms of working towards top pay.

There is anecdotal evidence that good information has already had some effect. There have for instance been several high-profile cases of women in broadcasting nego-tiating pay rises as a result of the BBC's declarations.[7] Their assumption is that big pay increases were brought about by their employer being unwilling to face another round of critical scrutiny for unacceptable or higher-than-aver-age pay differentials. The publication of reported pay gap figures has also stimulated women's groups and networks to collaborate to share better information. At one of the big banks an internal pay group has been meeting since the spring of 2018. There are, apparently, active female net-works sharing information in two of the big accountancy firms. These micro-networks are a positive result of gender pay gap reporting, and they will probably have a positive impact on equality of earnings, and on productivity.

What can organisations do about the gap?

That the part-time nature and longevity of women's careers have such a big impact on pay is undoubtedly related to childcare commitments. One of the reasons women take such a long time off looking after children is because child-care is too expensive. It doesn't make economic sense for most people to work and have their children looked after by other people if childcare costs outweigh their salaries, and there is only a slim chance that such investment will yield higher pay in the long run. Recently an ex-BBC journalist reported to the Work and Pensions Committee that she

---

7   BBC to reveal list showing increase in high-paid women, *The Guardian*, 11 July 2018 (https://www.theguardian.com/media/2018/jul/11/bbc-to-re veal-list-showing-increase-in-high-paid-women).

would only have had £60 a month left after childcare costs in London on a £32,000 salary.[8] If time out of the workplace damages women's earning prospects, and damages workplace equality, then it should perhaps be a policy goal for women to go back to work more quickly. A striking aspect of the childcare market is how little innovation and how few productivity changes there have been in it over the last two decades, compared to other labour-intensive services such as food services and medicine. There are many barriers to entry in the childcare market such as limits on the number of children carers can look after (Bourne and Shackleton 2017). For example, in Sweden and France carers can look after up to eight children per carer, but in England this number is only four, increased from three in 2013.

A higher proportion of women taking up flexible work is also a reason why women don't receive top pay. Research suggests that people working in jobs which offer flexibility pay a penalty for this. On the other hand, jobs where hours are long and commitment is required pay a significant premium. This can be readily seen in the long-hours culture that has emerged in the high-paying professions in the City, where hours in banking, finance, law and consultancy have soared in the last two decades. In jobs where hours and conditions have to be the same for all position holders, there is a smaller gender wage gap. This suggests that not

---

8   Universal Credit is 'women's human rights issue', ex-BBC journalist tells MPs after revealing she turned down £32,000 salary as it would leave her with £60-a-month after childcare, *Daily Mail*, 24 October 2018 (https://www.dailymail.co.uk/news/article-6312869/Universal-Credit-womens-human-rights-issue-ex-BBC-journalist-tells-MPs.html).

only do women pay a penalty for part-time working (Costa Dias et al. 2018), but that men earn a premium for being full time, and in high-paid occupations they earn what economists call a 'compensating differential' for being *more than* full time – constantly available and working long hours.

It might seem, therefore, that one route to closing the gender pay gap, and increasing women's participation at the top of the market, would be to offer flexible work for all, not just to parents.[9] One top law firm in the UK has offered flexible work to all employees at partner level. This is not applicable just to child caring but any reason for working flexibly. If men were to take up flexible working at the same rate as women do, it might be expected that the gender pay gap would fall. It is perhaps an idea to encourage – albeit with a light hand – companies that are able to offer flexible working to all to do so, if they want to see a smaller gender pay gap. But more work needs to be done to understand the barriers to flexible working for all, and whether employers and businesses are really getting maximum productivity from a long-hours culture or whether it is just needlessly perpetuating inequalities.

Quotas

There is evidence that policies favouring gender diversity have led, in some cases, to senior executive women being promoted more quickly than men, and that in such a highly qualified pool, in some locations being female actually

---

9   As argued for the similar American market by Goldin (2015).

increases the statistical chances of becoming CEO. However, a recent ILO report shows that while women hold 50 per cent of middle-management positions, less than 5 per cent of CEOs of publicly listed companies in OECD countries are women (just 2.8 per cent in the European Union) (International Labour Organization 2015). This is because, although a woman may have more of a chance when it comes to the executive board deciding the next CEO, there are significantly fewer women in the final pool in the first place.

The evidence on positive discrimination towards women, where quotas are used to balance board appointments, is surprisingly mixed. In Norway, for example, where they implemented corporate board quotas in 2003, the promotion of high-achieving women to public boards has done little to boost corporate performance or to change gendered business patterns elsewhere in the economy. One report notes that, seven years after the board quota policy fully came into effect, 'we conclude that it had very little discernible impact on women in business beyond its direct effect on the women who made it into boardrooms' (Bertrand et al. 2019: 191).

Conclusion

The current discourse around the gender pay gap tends to generalise the gap as discriminatory and unjust. The figures themselves and an understanding of labour markets as markets for information demonstrate that the problem is much more complex, and not something that can be easily, or fairly, legislated for. Different workplace behaviours and activities are the result of different choices and preferences, themselves gendered, arising from social and family roles and responsibilities which are the result of long-standing cultural institutions. Many of those cultural issues are undergoing rapid change among some groups, particularly among well-educated urban families where fathers are taking a much more active role. In general, however, much of the current difference in pay is the consequence of career patterns which are governed by women and men making different choices about how work and care-giving fit in with their lives. The evidence suggests that, apart from encouraging flexible work for all, legislating how employers behave and how they pay will not affect these things, except perhaps in unforeseen ways which may not help gender equality in the workplace or pay. Only by women's increased participation in work and in pay bargaining will pay become more equal.

If labour markets are markets for information, we should be optimistic because in 2018 the information available improved greatly. But we need to analyse that information properly within an understanding of how markets work rather than jump to hasty conclusions, or legislation. And the end goal should always be equality of opportunity, not equality of outcome.

8   PUBLIC SERVICE OR PUBLIC PLUNDER?

Alex Wild

It is relatively easy to dismiss concerns over high private sector pay as people are not forced to contribute to remuneration packages of private sector executives. If you have a moral disagreement with the amount a private sector employee is paid, you can usually choose to cease transacting with that individual or company. The same cannot be said of the public sector, which is largely funded by taxation which you must pay or face legal sanctions.

Definitional issues

There are, it should be said, several areas where distinctions between private and public sector are unclear. Parts of the public sector, such as Ordnance Survey and the Met Office, are run on a commercial basis and do not have any direct recourse to taxpayer funds. Likewise, there are some private sector companies (such as outsourcers Capita and G4S) and charities which are heavily, in some cases almost totally, reliant on government contracts. NHS General Practitioners are usually considered part of the public sector but are in reality private businesses, for example.

Put simply, there are people in the private sector paid almost exclusively with public money and people in the public sector paid almost exclusively with private money. This needs to be taken into consideration when trying to set hard and fast rules.

Who is better off?

Since 2010, much has been written about pay restraint in the public sector. What has often been referred to as a 'freeze' or a 'cap' has been restraint in increases of pay scale increments rather than a freeze on any individual's pay.

Leaving aside for a moment whether or not this is the optimal way in which to set public sector pay, it is important to consider how well public sector employees are paid relative to private sector employees as best we can. Table 5 sets out some basic comparisons. It shows clearly that the typical public sector worker is better paid than the typical private sector worker.

This table shows the figures without any context. People working in the public sector are on average better qualified than those in the private sector, and this needs to be borne in mind. After adjusting for characteristics such as education and experience, mean private sector pay actually overtook public sector pay in 2017, according to the Office for National Statistics.[1] This is, however, only part of the story, as the data exclude pensions.

---

1   Is pay higher in the public or private sector? Office for National Statistics, 16 November 2017 (https://www.ons.gov.uk/employmentandlabourmark et/peopleinwork/earningsandworkinghours/articles/ispayhigherinthe publicorprivatesector/2017-11-16).

Table 5   Gross weekly pay by percentile, 2017

Percentile	Public sector (£)	Private sector (£)	Difference in favour of public sector (%)
10	177.9	139.9	27
20	276.6	229.4	21
25	318.0	277.9	14
30	353.1	309.0	14
40	424.2	368.9	15
60	567.3	513.6	10
70	661.9	612.3	8
75	707.0	672.2	5
80	762.3	751.6	1
90	920.6	1,006.2	−9

Source: Office for National Statistics.

Table 6   Gross weekly pay within top decile, 2017

Percentile	Public sector (£)	Private sector (£)	Difference in favour of private sector (%)
90	920.6	1,006.2	9
91	949.3	1,054.1	11
92	985.8	1,105.8	12
93	1,026.4	1,158.7	13
94	1,075.2	1,235.0	15
95	1,128.0	1,317.2	17
96	1,206.8	1,424.1	18
97	1,319.9	1,571.9	19
98	1,535.6	1,812.1	18
99	1,934.6	2,232.1	15

Source: Office for National Statistics.

Table 6 looks in more detail at pay comparisons. Above the 90th percentile the gap in favour of the private sector increases to 19 per cent by the time we get to the 97th percentile.

At a superficial level, this could lead us to conclude that at the top end of the income distribution, public sector workers are relatively poorly paid compared to their private sector counterparts. However, even at a simple statistical level, such an argument doesn't stand up to scrutiny.

Pensions are far more generous in the public sector

As is the case across all income percentiles, gross pay figures fail to account for pensions. Pensions in the public sector are, almost exclusively, unfunded defined benefit schemes.[2] Such defined benefit schemes see employers bearing more risk as they guarantee to make pension payments to retirees at an agreed rate, irrespective of investment returns, if indeed any investments are made.

In funded schemes, assets are easy to value. They mainly consist of securities such as bonds and shares for which prices are regularly quoted. Liabilities are, however, far more difficult to value, depending on inflation, future investment performance and life expectancy. Accounting standards mandate that the discount rates used to value liabilities are based on high quality (AA) corporate bond

---

2   The biggest exception being local government pension schemes, which are partially funded defined benefit schemes.

yields. A prolonged period of low interest rates, such as we have been experiencing since the financial crisis, can therefore substantially increase a scheme's liabilities, at least in an accounting sense.

In the private sector, defined benefit schemes are effectively closed to new entrants. In 2016 there were just 58,000 private sector entrants into open defined benefit schemes.[3] The number of active members of open defined benefit schemes (i.e. those paying into them) in the private sector fell from 1.4 million to 0.5 million between 2006 and 2016.

The cost to the taxpayer of providing these old-style public sector pensions is extremely high. While employee contribution rates are higher, so are employer contributions. In the average open defined benefit scheme in 2016, employee contributions were 6.3 per cent but employer contributions were 15.6 per cent. On top of this, £12 billion was put into public sector schemes by the Treasury in 2017/18 to cover the shortfall between contributions and pension payments. Indeed the true costs of public sector defined benefit schemes are significantly understated as they use an artificial discount rate (Record 2014).

The contribution rate required by the most highly paid public sector workers varies significantly. For instance, a member of the NHS Pension Scheme earning a salary of £112,000 would be required to make a contribution of

3   Occupational Pension Schemes Survey, dataset, Office for National Statistics, 6 September 2018 (https://www.ons.gov.uk/peoplepopulationand community/personalandhouseholdfinances/pensionssavingsandinvest ments/datasets/occupationalpensionschemessurvey).

14.5 per cent,[4] but a member of the Civil Service Pension Scheme earning the same amount would only be required to contribute 7.35 per cent.[5] The Bank of England Pension Scheme requires no employee contributions at all. On average, public sector pensions are around five times as generous as those on offer in the private sector.[6]

These schemes have survived (albeit in a modestly reformed state) in the public sector for a number of reasons, financial and political. The state is not under the same financial constraints as private employers because it has the power to tax, and politicians make decisions for electoral rather than commercial reasons. The costs of providing these extremely generous pensions to public sector workers are both largely hidden from voters (as pension liabilities are excluded from public sector net debt figures quoted by Chancellors at budget time) and widely dispersed among taxpayers.

False comparisons

Various public sector bodies and unions have sought to make comparisons between the private and public sector

4 Pension contributions and tax arrangements, NHS Employers, 24 March 2017 (http://www.nhsemployers.org/your-workforce/pay-and-reward/pensions/pension-contribution-tax-relief#Employer).

5 Contribution Rates, Civil Service Pensions (https://www.civilservicepensionscheme.org.uk/members/contribution-rates/).

6 A nation divided: public sector pensions worth five times private sector pensions, Tilney Group, 24 February 2016 (https://group.tilney.co.uk/press/articles/a-nation-divided-public-sector-pensions-worth-five-times-private-sector-pensions).

in arguing for higher top pay. Granted, government departments, large local authorities and quangos are comparable to large businesses in terms of number of employees and revenues, but the similarities usually end there.

The best-paid people at such large public sector organisations are Permanent Secretaries and Chief Executives but they do not fulfil the same role as private sector chief executives. Local authorities and government departments do not operate in competitive conditions, have little or no responsibility for bringing new products and services to market, and are reliant on handouts from central government and/or taxes or charges they can levy.

Moreover, by and large, their employees implement instructions from elected politicians. They are, as Sir Humphrey Appleby would say, 'humble functionaries'.

Around 18,500 active companies became insolvent in 2017.[7] Public sector organisations on the other hand cease to exist only when the government of the day decides that it no longer wants them to exist. Such decisions are at least as political as they are financial, subject to considerable public scrutiny and are invariably met with considerable resistance from politicians, unions and user groups. The result is that public sector organisations are far less likely to make headcount reductions or close down altogether than private sector businesses. Poor decision-making by senior management does not result in falling revenues and job losses.

---

7   Insolvency statistics – October to December 2017 (Q4 2017), Insolvency Service, 26 January 2018 (https://assets.publishing.service.gov.uk/govern ment/uploads/system/uploads/attachment_data/file/675931/Insolvency _Statistics_-_web.pdf).

Granted, there is in principle scope for competition be-tween local authorities, but in practice there is currently very little autonomy with councils largely responsible for fulfilling over a thousand statutory duties. Competition between authorities is therefore minimal compared to other countries with greater devolution of responsibilities. Indeed, many politicians oppose more devolution on the grounds that it would create 'postcode lotteries' or start a 'race to the bottom' on service provision and local taxes.

Even in areas of the public sector where quasi-markets operate and providers compete with one another and can theoretically go bust (in some parts of the NHS and edu-cation), trusts and schools are seldom allowed to fail out-right and are instead bailed out or placed in some form of special measure or conservatorship. The roles of public sector headteachers and senior hospital managers and administrators are in some ways more similar to their private sector counterparts than the roles of, say, local authority chief executives are to private sector chief exec-utives: a hospital is responsible for treating patients and a school is responsible for teaching children, regardless of whether it is in the private sector or the public sector. But they remain significantly different owing to the far lower chance of their organisations failing and not being bailed out.

The need to compete with the private sector

High public sector pay is often justified by trade unions on the grounds that the public sector needs to compete with the private sector for top talent. While there are obvious risks if the public sector cannot recruit certain scarce skills and competences, the benefits of having public sector pay rates that persuade top talent to leave the private sector (or not enter it in the first place) have to be considered alongside the loss of their skills from the productive side of the economy. Almost all public sector workers are a net cost to the private sector and this net cost has to be paid for with tax revenues, present or future, which create deadweight losses.

There are greater similarities between public and private sector jobs in some roles rather than others. In lower-paid jobs such as basic administrative work for example, there are unlikely to be considerable differences between the skills required to work in the public sector or the private sector, nor are there likely to be significant differences between the nature of tasks employees are expected to perform. However, the most highly paid jobs in the private sector do not have an obviously analogous role in the public sector.

Regional differences

In some parts of the country, the problem is not one of the public sector's inability to recruit and retain workers, but rather the reverse, as Table 7 suggests. The loss of private sector talent to the public sector is exacerbated by national pay bargaining. While pay at the 90th percentile for the UK as a whole may be higher in the private sector than in the public sector, in some regions the reverse is true. Given that pay at the lower end of the public sector

Table 7   Regional pay differentials between public and private sectors, 2017

Region	Sector	Gross weekly pay (£)	Difference in favour of private sector (%)
North East	Public sector	845.7	1.9
	Private sector	861.6	
North West	Public sector	904.3	-2.7
	Private sector	879.7	
Yorkshire and The Humber	Public sector	830.7	1.7
	Private sector	845.2	
East Midlands	Public sector	856.6	0.4
	Private sector	860.2	
West Midlands	Public sector	860.8	6.3
	Private sector	915.1	
East	Public sector	890.9	7.6
	Private sector	958.2	
London	Public sector	1,149.7	33.4
	Private sector	1,533.2	
South East	Public sector	893.6	20.0
	Private sector	1,072.1	
South West	Public sector	854.9	2.5
	Private sector	876.1	
Wales	Public sector	858.1	-9.9
	Private sector	773	
Scotland	Public sector	890.6	4.4
	Private sector	929.6	

Source: Office for National Statistics.

is significantly higher than in the private sector, before even considering more generous annual leave, pensions and greater job security, higher public sector pay outside London and the South East must have a considerable crowding-out effect, leaving regions such as Wales and the North West reliant on transfers. For skilled workers in such regions, there is little incentive to work in the private sector.

Some difficult cases

Universities

The pay of university vice-chancellors has been the subject of significant public scrutiny and comment lately, largely owing to concerns over levels of tuition fees and student debt. This highly politically charged area provides a challenge to the analysis offered so far for a number of reasons.

On the one hand, universities are considered by some to be part of the public sector. They receive significant amounts of taxpayers' money both directly and in the form of tuition fees largely paid with taxpayer-subsidised loans and are covered by freedom of information legislation.

The Office for National Statistics classifies universities as 'Non-Profit Institutions Serving Households', together with such varied institutions as trade unions, political parties, religious organisations and charities. They are also not considered to be part of the public sector by the OECD – unlike in some other countries, where higher education is directly controlled by the state.

In contrast with most parts of the public sector, universities compete in a global marketplace for students and are far more freestanding than any other part of the public sector that springs to mind. There are also relatively few people capable of doing vice-chancellors' jobs and, despite their pay (sometimes in excess of £450,000 a year[8]) being very high in comparison to senior public sector employees, it is not obviously high compared to those who do the same job in other countries. Indeed, in the US and Australia many college presidents earn in excess of the equivalent of £1.5 million a year.

Furthermore, the skills and knowledge required to run a major university are far more transferable between countries than, say, those required to run a government department in another country with a different system of government and fundamentally different ways of delivering public goods and services. This issue is discussed further in the next chapter.

Medical professions

As with university vice-chancellors, the skills and qualifications of medical professionals are largely transferrable across borders. At the same time, one of the few advantages the NHS has over other developed countries' healthcare systems is that it is relatively easy for governments to constrain costs through more acute rationing and by restraining pay. The result is that hospital doctors in the

---

8   £500,000-a-year London Business School don puts £1 bag of M&S crisps on his expenses, *Daily Mail*, 20 January 2019 (https://www.dailymail.co.uk/news/article-6612739/500-000-year-London-Business-School-don-puts-1-bag-M-S-crisps-expenses.html).

UK are relatively lowly paid compared to hospital doctors in comparable countries,[9] despite being among the highest-paid public sector workers.

The BBC

Another area in which top pay has received national attention is the BBC. Some of this attention has been in response to perceived discrimination and has taken the form of, for example, comparing the pay of the female China editor with that of the male US editor.[10] Such comparisons are arguably invalid considering the markedly different attitudes to press freedom and viewers' interest levels in these countries, but this issue is beyond the scope of this chapter.

However, the wider furore has led to disclosures of top pay, with 'stars' such as Gary Lineker and Chris Evans being paid in excess of £1.5 million a year and newsreaders and current affairs programme presenters being paid up to £500,000.

In some of these areas, the BBC does undoubtedly compete for talent with commercial broadcasters such as ITV and Sky. Indeed, the BBC has tried to defend generous pay packages by pointing to the higher amounts earned by presenters on channels such as Sky Sports. However, it

9   Health at a glance 2017, OECD iLibrary, 10 November 2017 (https://www.oecd-ilibrary.org/social-issues-migration-health/health-at-a-glance-2017_health_glance-2017-en#page=159).

10 BBC China editor Carrie Gracie quits post in equal pay row, BBC News, 8 January 2018 (https://www.bbc.co.uk/news/uk-42598775).

is not obvious why the BBC should be trying to compete with commercial broadcasters given that it is primarily a public service broadcaster funded by what is in effect a poll tax.

Furthermore, public suspicion that some BBC staff are overpaid has been confirmed by the voluntary pay cuts some have taken in response to the public uproar.[11]

Bailed-out companies

The government's response to the financial crisis involved the state taking a majority shareholding in a number of financial institutions, most (in)famously Royal Bank of Scotland, Lloyds and Northern Rock. In the wake of these bailouts, senior management was removed and replaced with new executives. The pay of bankers is much commented on and, with the transfer of the employees of these institutions to the public sector, has become a much more political issue.

It could be argued that, as majority shareholders, taxpayers should have a role in determining the compensation levels of senior executives at such institutions as RBS; however, the practicalities of giving this responsibility to the public make it impossible. While the government clearly has a duty to rein in excess at government-owned institutions, there are difficult questions as to where its role should begin and end.

---

11 BBC pay: John Humphrys says he will earn 'hugely less', BBC News, 26 January 2018 (https://www.bbc.co.uk/news/entertainment-arts-42840517).

And unlike previous examples, bailed-out banks are in unequivocally direct competition with the private sector. Ultimately, it is in taxpayers' long-term interest that bailed-out companies are commercially successful and they are less likely to be so if senior executive pay levels are similar to those in the civil service.

Charities

Charities provide another challenge. Along with the significant tax benefits of charitable status bestowed by the state, large numbers of charities are heavily,[12] in some cases almost entirely (Norton 2014), dependent on the state for their income. This blurs the line between public and private sectors, raising legitimate questions as to how some charities should be categorised. High pay at charities has been the subject of much negative media coverage in recent years, and major concerns have been raised about large charities' governance and auditing[13] standards. Unlike most parts of the public sector, however, they can be, and have been, allowed to fail like

---

12 The 27,000 charities that survive on taxpayers' cash and lobby for the pet causes of politicians, Institute of Economic Affairs, 11 June 2012 (https:// iea.org.uk/in-the-media/media-coverage/the-27000-charities-that -survive-on-taxpayers-cash-and-lobby-for-the-pet).

13 Accounts monitoring: Concerns highlighted by auditors in their audit reports 2017, Charity Commission for England and Wales, 15 March 2018 (https://www.gov.uk/government/publications/accounts-monitoring -concerns-highlighted-by-auditors-in-their-audit-reports-2017/ac counts-monitoring-concerns-highlighted-by-auditors-in-their-audit -reports-2017).

private companies dependent on the state for the bulk of their income.

Conclusions

While it's clear that pay levels at the very top of the private sector are higher than they are at the top of the public sector, people employed in senior roles in each sector perform fundamentally different roles. Poor decisions made by private sector executives can result in the demise of the companies they manage but the same is rarely if ever true in the public sector. The making of high-level decisions in the public sector is usually the responsibility of politicians rather than top officials.

Rigidity of pay scales and national pay bargaining mean there is little variation in top public sector pay regionally, and between well and poorly performing public sector organisations. That said, it is often difficult to assess the performance of many public sector organisations which do not produce goods and services that have a market value.[14]

There are a number of challenging areas, however, which do not fit into a simple public versus private distinction. It is sometimes difficult to find clear justification for such organisations being linked to the public sector at all, unless as a temporary measure. If they were clearly in the private sector and fully exposed to market forces, high pay issues should not be of any concern to the general public.

---

14 Indeed, some public sector activities could be argued to have a negative value.

And in areas where it is less clear-cut that organisations should be in the private sector, such as schools and hospitals, there is considerable scope for them to be exposed to greater market discipline which might allay some concerns over high pay.

9 ARE VICE-CHANCELLORS PAID TOO MUCH?

Rebecca Lowe

Introduction

Concern over high pay is not confined to growing attention on business executives with multimillion-pound salaries and generous pensions. The individuals running the UK's ever-expanding higher education sector have also received considerable negative publicity of late. Although vice-chancellors (VCs) – who are essentially chief executives with extra status and obligations – are paid rather more modestly than their corporate counterparts, accusations of exploitation abound from all sides.

The government has responded to concerns about VC pay by affording a new regulatory body, the Office for Students (OfS), the power to monitor and publish VCs' remuneration packages, and to require universities to provide 'detailed justifications' for these packages, including consideration of pay ratios. This chapter explores the situation and arguments in detail.

The costs and value of the higher education sector

Although a substantial Higher Education and Research Act received Royal Assent in 2017,[1] and a new review[2] is currently under way, clarity has often been missing from public discussion about the UK's provision of post-18 education. Obfuscation has driven cynicism and impaired the general understanding of policies, not least those related to fees and funding. Meanwhile, important questions relating to the existing and normative role of higher education (HE) remain overlooked. Arguments about pay, and particularly that of HE's top executives, typify this problem. Fundamental questions need serious deliberation before the remuneration of those executives can be addressed, not least because top pay rates do not occur in a vacuum.

Universities are highly bureaucratic, complex, growing systems, often supporting thousands of students and employees – and they are highly varied. Recognising variety is key to understanding the sector: all universities are not the same; neither should we expect their employees to be the same, or to be paid the same. Many types of institution sit under the umbrella of 'university'; in the UK, the word largely equates to what other countries tend to call

1 Higher Education and Research Act 2017 (https://www.legislation.gov.uk/id/ukpga/2017/29).

2 Prime Minister launches major review of post-18 education, Department for Education, 19 February 2018 (https://www.gov.uk/government/news/prime-minister-launches-major-review-of-post-18-education).

'the tertiary education sector'. While all UK universities provide HE, all providers of UK HE are not universities. Meanwhile, even the institutions referred to as 'universities' are highly disparate, in terms of parameters ranging from purpose, to results, to size, and more.

The number of students participating in UK HE grew dramatically over the twentieth century,[3] in line with changes of attitude and policy. In 1920, just 4,357 people gained an undergraduate degree. By 1950, this had risen to 17,337. There was relatively little change by 1960, but over 50,000 graduated in 1970. Numbers continued to grow gradually, before a notable change at the end of the century. In 1990, 77,163 gained undergraduate degrees; in 2000, this had risen to 243,246 – an increase of 215 per cent in just ten years. Numbers have continued to increase since, and are now around 400,000 annually.

Extended provision has been driven by a desire to equalise: to try to ensure that everyone suited and keen to pursue a university education is able to attain one. There are flaws in any expansion-based approach to achieving this admirable goal, however, and an equalising approach has not only branded all students (or, often, more accurately, all 18-year-olds) the same, it has also done the same for HE establishments.

Financial commitment has been central to government involvement in HE over the last century. With the sector's growth has come increased expense and new

---

3   Education: Historical statistics, House of Commons Library, November 2012 (http://researchbriefings.parliament.uk/ResearchBriefing/Summary/SN 04252#fullreport).

approaches to funding, as well as changing attitudes to the extent to which the state should be involved.[4] The Treasury estimates 2018 HE spending at £17.3 billion (Institute for Fiscal Studies 2018: 65). However, while expense has been gradually transferred to graduates and direct funding reduced, the cost to the taxpayer of student loans remains extensive. The Institute for Fiscal Studies (Crawford et al. 2014) calculated in 2014 that for each £1 loaned, the 'long-run cost' to the government was 43.3p (this cost has now risen since the earnings of a larger proportion of graduates have fallen below a higher repayment threshold). £17.7 billion of HE providers' current £35.7 billion income comes from fees.

An awareness of the intrinsic and instrumental value of the teaching and learning of knowledge has always been behind state support of the HE sector. The economic value of university education – to graduates and wider society – is well-documented (see, for example, Oxford Economics 2017). It is also essential to recognise the wider value HE brings in terms of a shared democratic and deliberative pay-off. Martha Nussbaum has championed 'the case for liberal arts education, in connection with democratic citizenship', criticising how related skills acquired from studying humanities and arts subjects are often seen by

---

4   All but five of Britain's universities are currently completely government regulated, and partly publicly funded. Although these 'public' institutions are responsible for their staff (who are not civil servants, as is often the case in Europe), and have their own assets, their research and teaching standards are externally regulated, as are their funding and fee-setting arrangements.

policymakers as 'useless frills', unrelated to 'stay[ing] competitive in the global market'.[5]

The setting of VC pay

Universities' societal obligations seem extensive, owing to both the educative nature of their purpose and the privileged place they hold in society – not least regarding the taxpayer support they receive. For many people, this brings certain expectations about the remuneration of HE employees, and leads to criticisms about the escalating pay rates of VCs. Of course, these kinds of expectations are not limited to discussions of higher education (Lucas 2013):

> How much should the Queen be paid? There is no market in Queens, and if there were, it would be impracticable to choose between the many would-be Queens who had offered themselves. Although there are many jobs that can be left to the market to sort out, there are others where some social consensus is needed about appropriate levels of pay.

Agreeing with Lucas does not equate to suggesting that the state – or some kind of bureaucratic people's tribunal – should determine the levels of pay for those jobs about which 'some social consensus is needed', however. In the case of VCs, it seems appropriate for universities to

---

5   The education crisis and the depletion of democracy, ABC Religion and Ethics, 15 February 2011 (http://www.abc.net.au/religion/articles/2011/02/15/3139497.htm).

recognise and choose to meet their own societal obligations. But if being a VC is indeed an example of such a job – and, for the purpose of this investigation, we might take it to be – then how should current rates of pay be assessed? Are pay ratios relevant? Whether a VC is 'worth' x times as much as a y depends not only on the extent to which we value y, but also whether we think such crude comparisons are helpful.

There are three main issues that are in need of consideration when assessing pay rates: what they are, how they came to be so, and whether what they are is right – and 'right' could be grounded on ideas of market freedom, efficiency, fairness, or other factors. That the UK has a minimum wage, the introduction and setting of which was predicated on concepts such as need and fairness, means that pay at the bottom end of most sectors is standardised and regulated. This has detrimental effects on the flexibility of the labour market in terms of compressing pay differentials, and can be particularly problematic for lower-skilled workers and small businesses. In certain industries, the high degree of influence of trade unions and other industry bodies also has a direct impact on pay rates.

John Hicks's *The Theory of Wages* (1932, 1963) remains one of the best accounts for understanding how pay works in a competitive market. Wages, Hicks explains, are 'the price of labour; and thus, in the absence of control, are determined, like all prices, by supply and demand'. However, he points out that, although a simple supply–demand model of pay works well in descriptive terms, its explanatory powers are lacking (ibid.: 4–5):

> Wages, say the text-books, tend to that level where demand and supply are equal. [...] Now this, as I hope to make abundantly clear, is quite a good simplified model of the labour market. [...] But, since it is a simplified model, it is extremely likely to be misconstrued by those who take it to be an account of how the real labour market works.

Hicks explains that, in order to understand phenomena such as unemployment, it is necessary to recognise that the determination of wages is a 'special case' of the general theory of value: the demand for labour is a *derived* demand, that is, it is generally what the labour produces that is valued rather than the labour itself.

For expository purposes, Hicks uses a static equilibrium model to set out his general principles. But in truth the labour market is ever changing, because, as he explains, its economic determiners are (ibid.: 18):

> changes in tastes, changes in knowledge, changes in the natural environment, and in the supply and efficiency of the factors of production generally. As these things change, so the marginal productivity of labour changes, and these changes in marginal productivity exert pressure in one direction or other on the level of wages.

Hicks builds on previous work, including that of Alfred Marshall (1890), in emphasising how the principle of marginal productivity is central to explicating wage setting, but he points out that the market is insufficiently flexible

– owing to factors such as investment in fixed capital – to allow for rapid adaptations to the level of wages following significant changes in the marginal productivity of labour.

Now, if the general labour market is special and complex in these senses, then surely the HE labour market is even more so? It is not only that the latter is affected by the standard factors Hicks emphasises, including the minimum wage and the rigidity that comes with a focus on cost-effectiveness in the investment of large amounts of public capital. The salaries of HE's lower-to-mid-range-paid employees are also, in large part, determined by national pay scales, and, at the very top end, there are a fixed number of jobs: one VC per university.[6]

Regarding the setting of VCs' pay, it is important to recognise the difference between the majority of the sector, which receives public funds (on which this chapter focuses), and alternative providers. Publicly funded universities are guided on issues of remuneration by the Committee of University Chairs (CUC) – and, most importantly, by the CUC's HE Code of Governance, its note on remuneration committees, and its recent Remuneration Code (Committee of University Chairs 2014, 2015, 2018). The aim of the Remuneration Code, published in June 2018, is to inspire good practice; the CUC claims that governing bodies that 'visibly adopt' this code will be 'demonstrat[ing] leadership and stewardship in relation to remuneration within their institutions'. Rather than making specific

---

6   New alternative providers will enter the market – and at an increased rate, following the changes set forth in the recent HE Act – but it will take time for this to have any real effect on wages.

recommendations on ranges of appropriate pay, the code focuses on the abstract concepts of fairness, transparency and independence. Institutions abiding by the code are required, however, to publish an annual statement, including information such as their 'choice of comparator institutions/organisations', the 'pay multiple of the HoI[7] and the median earnings of the institution's whole workforce', and 'an explanation of any significant changes'.

Each university has a remuneration committee, which determines and oversees the pay and conditions of senior staff. The membership of these committees often includes VCs or their equivalent, although the majority of members are expected to be 'lay governors' (who are not in the pay of the university), and VCs are also expected to leave the room when their own pay is discussed. Senior pay is usually set in terms of a base salary, although a number of institutions give performance-related bonuses, via systems of varying clarity – some based on quantitative metrics, and others on qualitative assessments of achievements. Moreover, transparency in the system as a whole unsurprisingly sometimes leads to universities increasing their senior staff's remuneration when they learn that competitor institutions are paying significantly more.

A few other factors should be noted. Recently, significant changes have taken place in the distribution of many VCs' pay: for their tax benefit, the balance between salary and pension has varied. While such changes do not alter the overall cost to institutions, they do affect headline

7   Head of Institution.

figures. It is also well documented that some VCs took voluntary pay freezes during the Great Recession, and it is also sometimes claimed that VCs make sizeable donations to student welfare programmes, and other similar enterprises. If we were to consider acts of charity as relevant to justifying pay rates, however, surely that would effectively be to argue that distributing funds differently in the first place – cutting senior pay, and spending the difference on such programmes – would be a better approach. Finally, once again, differences in the sector are key. The highest-paid individuals in institutions with medical and business schools – where rates are driven up by externally determined clinical pay, or the benefits that strong connections with big business can bring – are not always VCs, but VC pay is pushed up relatively, nonetheless.

The headline finding of the 2018 annual Times Higher Education survey is that average VC remuneration (salary, bonuses, and benefits) rose by 3.9 per cent in 2016/17, to £268,103 – or, when pension contributions are included, to £289,756 (an increase of 3.2 per cent). Median VC pay for 2016/17 was £261,289, or £287,000 including pensions, and VCs' total remuneration including pension costs is shown to range from £136,000 to £808,000. The top figure is an outlier, however, owing to a 'pay-off for loss of office'; the next highest amount is £471,000. The University and College Union (UCU) also publishes annual reports into VC pay.[8] These reports, which depend partly on Freedom of Information requests, reveal (most) VCs' salaries; the rates

---

8   Transparency at the top? University and College Union, 25 May 2018
     (https://www.ucu.org.uk/vcpay).

of increase in those salaries; the extent of VCs' expenses, including property, spend on air fares, accommodation and consultancy fees; and the pay, and pay increases, of their staff. UCU also requests the minutes of universities' remuneration committee meetings.

Is current VC pay 'right'?

To attempt to assess whether current VC pay rates are appropriate, it seems sensible first to consider what being a VC might entail. Disparity in pay between VCs is more easily explicable if they are carrying out highly varied duties. But what are those duties, and are they being fulfilled? If they are, are VCs rewarded fairly? If not, are they held accountable? Do the disparities between pay and role, or performance, match? And how else might we assess whether the system is working efficiently, whether it is fair, and whether pay sends the right message?

Few VCs are as distinguished as the Australian National University's 2015 appointment: Brian Schmidt has not only won a Nobel Prize, he also runs a famous vineyard. It is worth noting at this point that Schmidt, with a salary of around $618,000 (or £360,000), was, in June 2017, 'likely among the lowest paid of all Australian vice-chancellors, despite [ANU] being among the highest-ranked in the country', according to *The Australian*.[9] While few match

9   Nobel-winning ANU V-C Brian Schmidt is one of our worst-paid, *The Australian*, 15 June 2017 (http://www.theaustralian.com.au/higher-educa tion/nobelwinning-anu-vc-brian-schmidt-is-one-of-our-worstpaid/news -story/ee31bbb84adbbf2516f45530ee776317).

Schmidt's eminence, many UK VCs have held prominent positions – in the public and charity sectors, on powerful committees, advisory councils, and more. And nearly all high-ranking universities demand strong academic credentials in their leaders (although an increasing number of VCs come from more practical academic backgrounds, such as business or engineering). But whether the heads of universities should be successful academics, as well as good ambassadors, depends again on what it is their job entails.

VCs' duties vary widely depending on factors such as the size, prestige and aims of their university, yet the following statements relate to most holders of the position: the VC is a university's principal academic and administrative officer, its chief executive and often the chair of its primary academic body and a member of its governing body; the VC determines their university's 'strategic direction' and must maintain and build on its reputation, not least its place in league tables; the VC usually has responsibility for thousands of staff, and a sizeable financial turnover (for instance, the University of Warwick's is £0.6 billion);[10] the VC also has regulatory responsibilities, performs a ceremonial and civic role, and creates and maintains business and governmental partnerships in the UK and abroad.

One former university executive describes running a university as being 'similar to running a small town' – not only is it effectively the biggest hotel in the area, its leaders

---

10 Finance, Warwick University (https://warwick.ac.uk/about/profile/finan ce/).

also have to provide local leadership on issues ranging from environmental impact to terrorism. Universities might be said to be public *authorities* rather than public *bodies*, which raises the level of risk involved for their leaders. As the sector has become more competitive and international, a greater degree of risk and complexity has also arisen. Closer to home, VCs' engagement with external bodies also includes dealing with multiple trade unions. Again, however, it is clear that these demands vary greatly depending on the specific institution.

When asked to justify the level of VCs' pay in terms of what they actually do – rather than by making comparisons between their pay and the pay of others in or out of the sector – VCs often emphasise the (large) size of their institution and the (high) quality of its achievements. It is, they claim, a huge responsibility to run such a place. Significant correlations are often assumed, therefore, between pay and performance, and pay and size. Although it would theoretically be possible to compare performance changes against pay changes, there are so many complicating factors (differing lengths of tenure; the time it takes for a VC to effect change; shifts in pay composition; universities falling down the rankings not because their performance has worsened, but because other universities' performance has improved; external financial problems; and so on) that this does not seem worthwhile.

The extent to which any pay–performance link can be made also depends not only on the duties of the VC – and the extent to which those duties have been successfully completed – but also, again, on the way in which university performance is judged. Within the standard rankings, performance is assessed in a complex manner, taking all kinds of, sometimes subjective, factors into consideration. And many of the standard factors could be challenged – for instance, high spending on services could imply inefficiencies. This returns us to a discussion about purpose: to determine whether an institution is successful, it is necessary first to decide what it is it should be doing. To determine whether a leader is successful depends partly on that prior decision, and partly on the extent to which the leader has had (or is seen to have had) a positive effect in that way. That UK HE institutions are so varied makes it extremely difficult to compare and rank them. If institutions have different aims, they should be judged according to those aims.

As well as performance, it is also useful to take size of institution into account. Size is a less subjective distinction than performance, but a small highly specialised institution will have different aims from a small 'average' one, and bigger institutions will have certain advantages – not least economies of scale – that might make it seem inappropriate or inefficient to pay their VCs substantially more. Relying upon arguments such as 'my university is very big' or 'my university is near the top of x league table' is clearly insufficient.

It is often argued that high VC pay is justified because VCs are players in a competitive market covering over 100 countries, and that UK VCs receive substantially lower average pay than their counterparts in America and Australia. But it is hard to know how many UK VCs have received offers to move to competitor institutions abroad, and how many would genuinely consider such a move; it is also clear that certain UK institutions provide a much bigger draw than others when attempting to attract top candidates from abroad. It is also important to recognise international variety. As there are significant differences within the UK system, there are also significant differences between (and within) international systems – not least when comparing the UK with the US, where VCs' equivalents have, typically, been more involved in fundraising and alumni relations, and where there is a clear distinction between public and private colleges.

According to the *Chronicle of Higher Education*, the eight highest-paid US private university presidents earned $2,000,000 or more in 2014, and the highest earned $5,449,405 (around £4,108,000).[11] In 2015, the eight highest paid US public university presidents earned $1,000,000 or more.[12] In August 2017, *The Australian* reported that, in 2016, average public university VC pay in Australia had risen to $890,000, that eleven VCs earned over $1,000,000, that the highest paid earned $1,385,000 (around £817,000), and that pay at the 38 relevant institutions ranged from $225,000 to $1,385,000.[13] The highest-paid South African

11 The highest-paid private college presidents, *Forbes*, 5 December 2016 (https://www.forbes.com/sites/karstenstrauss/2016/12/05/the-highest -paid-private-college-presidents/#201d4710444e).

12 The highest-paid public university presidents, *Forbes*, 17 July 2017 (https:// www.forbes.com/sites/laurensonnenberg/2017/07/17/the-top-paid-pub lic-university-presidents/#42a9feca114c).

13 Uni vice-chancellors' average salary package hits $890,000, *The Australian*, 5 August 2017.

VC (of the universities revealing VC pay rates) is the head of Stellenbosch University, currently on a salary of R4.5 million (around £260,000).[14]

That UK VCs earn markedly less than their counterparts in the US, and somewhat less than their counterparts in Australia, does not in itself justify their levels of pay: it may be the case that their counterparts abroad earn far too much. After all, there is ongoing criticism of South African VCs, who, on average, earn significantly less. Moreover, once again, it is important to remember the many differences between these institutions – and their locations – not least concerning living costs, and levels of public funding.

Another approach often taken in assessing UK VC pay involves employing comparisons with other UK sectors. In September 2017, Louise Richardson, VC of the University of Oxford, was widely criticised for attempting to justify her pay by claiming she earned less than footballers. If she was referring specifically to the average pay of Premier League footballers, then, at least, she was correct: the Global Sports Salary Survey 2017 reported this to be £2.4 million per year;[15] the *Daily Express* calculated that Premier League team averages ranged from £954,000 (Burnley) to

---

14 SA's cash-strapped universities pay bosses multimillion-rand salaries, *Sunday Times* (South Africa), 11 November 2018 (https://www.timeslive.co.za/news/south-africa/2018-11-11-sas-cash-strapped-universities-pay-bosses-multimillion-rand-salaries/).

15 Global Sports Salaries Survey 2016 (https://www.globalsportssalaries.com/GSSS%202016.pdf).

£5.77 million (Manchester United), at the time.[16] However, players in the lower leagues do not command anywhere near the same amounts as Premier League stars. But are these comparisons in any sense relevant? In that there is only a small, relatively fixed number of jobs both in the Premier League and at the top of UK universities' managerial structures, there are some similarities. It is harder, however, to think of ways in which the duties of the people in these very different jobs might correspond.

Which jobs might be more suited to comparisons with VCs, then? Ministers? Judges? Heads of NHS trusts? And, if we accept that universities have many of the same obligations as businesses, then how are VCs paid in comparison with CEOs? If pay ratios are, in any sense, relevant in terms of wider societal fairness, then what can we take from the fact that the average VC is paid almost ten times more than the average UK worker?

Research by the Equality Trust (2017) analysed the 2015 annual reports and accounts of all FTSE-100 companies and found that average pay for the CEOs of these companies was £5,217,803. That figure is almost 200 times higher than average UK pay, and the Trust reported it to be 165 times more than a nurse's pay and 312 times more than that of a care worker. The bigger the differentiation within the pay of those doing a certain job, the less directly useful

---

16 Premier League wages confirmed: how much did every team spend last season? *Daily Express*, 8 May 2017 (http://www.express.co.uk/sport/foot ball/801919/Premier-League-wages-confirmed-Man-United-sportgaller ies).

this information is, but using the same approach, the average pay of a FTSE-100 CEO is 20 times more than the average pay of a VC. Comparing VC salaries with executive pay rates in schools might be more appropriate, however, not least owing to the public nature of the VC role, and any special expectations we might have for those in the field of education. Headteachers, who are paid on an official scale, which currently ranges from £45,213 to £111,007 (excluding London weighting), clearly earn much less than VCs.[17] Considering the relative scales of enterprise, however, comparisons with the CEOs of multi-academy trusts (MATs) might be more relevant. The highest-paid MAT head earned £420,000 in 2016, a figure not dissimilar to the highest-paid UK VC, but this particular MAT role is generally taken as an understandable outlier.[18] *Schools Week* reported in March 2017 that the average pay across the twelve largest academy trusts was £210,000, however – again, not much lower than average VC pay.[19]

Other points of comparison include the following: the average earnings for an NHS chief executive in 2016 were £172,000;[20] the highest 'salary group' on the April 2017 Ministry of Justice 'Judicial Salaries' scale was £252,079, and

---

17 See: https://www.nasuwt.org.uk/uploads/assets/uploaded/e2c3ba3f-20f3-410c-ae4b83329cbe3e4a.pdf

18 The Harris Foundation is one of the biggest and most successful MATs.

19 Academy CEO pay: salaries soar, but who comes out on top? *Schools Week*, March 2017 (https://schoolsweek.co.uk/academy-ceo-pay-salaries-soar-but-who-comes-out-on-top/).

20 For example: NHS nurses, midwives, managers and directors pay scales for 2016/2017, Hospital Dr (http://www.hospitaldr.co.uk/blogs/guidance/nurses-and-nhs-managers-pay-scales).

the lowest, £108,171;[21] the Prime Minister's pay is currently £153,907; and, since April 2018, the basic annual salary for MPs has been £77,397.[22] Many executives receive considerable expense allowances and extra benefits on top of their salaries, however; an employee's salary is not their entire cost to their employer. Nonetheless, these basic comparators are interesting. But what more than novelty can we take from the findings that the average VC earns significantly less than the average FTSE CEO or Premier League footballer, about the same as a judge in the highest MoJ salary group, and somewhat more than the Prime Minister or an NHS chief executive? Again, we would first need to assess what it is we expect from people holding those positions, and also – if fundamental justification is the aim – whether it is right that anyone earns such an extreme amount more than the average income in their society.

Two main themes re-emerge: purpose and variety. Dealing in averages is clearly unhelpful – there is vast variety within and without the HE sector. And we must also remember special expectations we might have for those in public roles, particularly when those roles are supported by public funding, or have a link to education. Any useful assessment of pay in the HE sector must be grounded with an awareness of these themes of purpose and variety. And so should any exploration

---

21 Judicial salaries and fees: 2016 to 2017, Ministry of Justice, 21 April 2016 (https://www.gov.uk/government/publications/judicial-salaries-and -fees-2016-to-2017).

22 See, for example: Pay and expenses for MPs, Parliament (https://www .parliament.uk/about/mps-and-lords/members/pay-mps/).

of the application of pay ratios in general. If a pay-ratio approach is deemed appropriate regarding VCs, then, surely, to be consistent, similar considerations should be extended more widely: to the CEOs of private sector companies receiving large amounts of public funding, for instance – and, particularly, those within the education sector (such as the companies providing technical services and resources in schools, which are paid for out of school budgets). This seems extremely problematic for many reasons, not least the extraordinary effort it would require, but it is the logical conclusion – or potential unintended consequence – of such an approach.

Perhaps more significantly, it is often asked whether it is 'right' that so much money is spent on VC pay when many early-career academics struggle with low pay and the often precarious nature of their employment. Is pay throughout the sector fair? Are administrative roles valued more highly than academic roles? In May 2017, *Times Higher Education* reported that, in 2015/16, the overall mean average full-time salary for the sector was £40,449, that the average pay of staff on academic contracts was £49,908, and that the average pay for professors was £79,030.[23] Again, it must be recognised that these average remuneration rates are partly tied to a national pay scale. The Single Pay Spine – which is nationally agreed via negotiations between the Joint Negotiating Committee for Higher Education Staff (JNCHES) and the Universities

---

23 *Times Higher Education* also published a list of the institutions with the highest professorial salaries, as well as various pay gap calculations (by both gender and ethnicity).

and Colleges Employers Association (UCEA) – covers most UK HE institutions: 148 universities are represented in the annual negotiations. From August 2017, the national spine ranged from £15,417 to £60,410. Universities publish their own frameworks, which match the national spine, but are divided into pay grades, as no national grades are set. Pay grades differ between institutions, not least so institutions can respond to their local market, and supplement basic pay to remain competitive. London weighting (inner, outer, and fringe) is also nationally agreed, and applied by relevant institutions, with a division between pre- and post-92 institutions. Universities also typically set professorial pay scales. Most institutions offer discretionary extras throughout, respond to bargaining, and professors can often negotiate super-payments. Different universities have different systems, and it is worth remembering that a mid-career academic at a small, low-ranked university might earn more than someone at a comparable stage at Oxbridge – not least because Oxford and Cambridge can rely partly on knowing that academics will always be drawn to working there.[24]

Most universities also employ some academics on hourly-paid rates. It seems generally understood within the sector that, although individual experiences differ vastly, working as an early-career or part-time academic can be

---

24 Pay is only one factor determining the attractiveness of a job; prestige is another. Thus pay, other things being equal, may be expected to show an inverse relationship to the relative attractiveness of working at different universities. This is the principle of 'compensating differentials', which goes back to *The Wealth of Nations* by Adam Smith.

precarious and financially straining.[25] In response to such criticism, universities often claim that the ending of the awarding of block grants has brought instability to the sector, as there is no longer a steady income stream. It is also emphasised that it remains the case that researchers apply for projects or fellowships for a fixed number of years (the average salary for these jobs is within the £30,000–£40,000 bracket). Now that more students go on to doctoral study, competition is fierce, even though there are increasing numbers of institutions and posts. And policy changes throughout the wider education system can also cause volatility between subjects.

The future

Any need for a change of attitude towards pay or employment practices at the bottom end does not necessarily equate to a need for reforms at the top end, however. Reducing pay at the top is sometimes assumed to provide a quick route to improving overall finances, but the amounts saved, even by substantially cutting VCs' pay, would not go far in increasing the salaries of those at the bottom.[26] There

---

25 See, for example, UCU analysis within: 2017/18 Joint Higher Education Trade Union Pay Claim, Unison, 22 March 2017 (https://www.unison.org.uk/news/article/2017/03/higher-education-unions-submit-2017-18-pay-claim/); and: The rise of academic ill-health, Wonkhe blog, 5 September 2017 (http://wonkhe.com/blogs/the-rise-of-academic-ill-health/).

26 Similarly, claims that increased tuition fees are being used to raise VCs' salaries are also somewhat trite: one university executive claims that each student would only need to contribute £4.80 per year to pay their VC's salary in full.

is also the serious fear of unintended consequences. The most obvious concern related to reducing VC pay – aside from unease about who it would be that would drive or enforce this reduction – is that the regulation or capping of executive pay would hinder institutions' attempts to attract the highest calibre candidates.

However, it is clear that universities could benefit in certain ways from addressing remuneration from top to bottom, and that they should be made aware of such potential gains. Even though there is little to suggest that increased pay at the top of a society or organisation has a detrimental economic effect on those further down the distribution, there are other factors to consider. Legitimate questions remain regarding distributional equality's instrumental value, in fostering social goods such as happiness, for instance. Paying VCs less might not have much effect economically, but resultant benefits to the sector – and the value of its societal messaging – could be substantial. And, given that most universities remain largely 'public' institutions, it does not seem inappropriate for citizens to have an interest in the remuneration of HE executives, not least because the sector continues to have a significant dependence on general taxation. If universities were to choose to reduce executive pay – or, at least, to choose to clarify and justify their decision-making more transparently in cases of particularly high pay, as requested by the Committee of University Chairs – this could also send a unifying message to their students and employees, and particularly those facing financial hardship or insecurity related to their studies or employment.

Finally, it is clear that, rather than continued governmental tinkering around the edges of highly publicised HE problems, such as fees and funding, some systemic faults could be addressed with a formal segmentation of tertiary education, to allow for a greater degree of specialisation and competition. Treating all HE providers the same in terms of our expectations and the way in which their performance is judged is inefficient and societally detrimental – not least regarding the stretching of funding, and the disadvantage faced by potential students who are less informed about the relative merits of institutions. The sector is currently so over-extended, complex, and governmentally and bureaucratically driven that it is impossible to hope that fighting for the space for standard economically liberal principles to hold sway could lead to much improvement without serious change first, particularly in terms of funding. This may seem defeatist, but it is hardly surprising that half-hearted attempts to increase competition in the setting of fees have failed. A substantial rethink is long overdue.

Nonetheless, as long as universities remain to any extent dependent on the taxpayer it is hard not to conclude that we should have special expectations regarding the way in which they are run, and that there is a particular public interest in their spending and other financial activities.

10 GETTING TOUGH ON TOP PAY: WHAT CONSEQUENCES?

J. R. Shackleton

Politicians from Theresa May to Jeremy Corbyn, and commentators of many different persuasions, think that something should be done to rein in high pay in UK business. They don't always spell out exactly what this 'something' should be. If they do, little is said about the possible negative consequences of policy interventions.[1] In this contribution I look at some proposed policies and outline possible knock-on effects.

Publishing pay ratios and 'naming and shaming'

In its 2017 Corporate Governance green paper the government proposed publishing CEO pay ratios and supporting explanations, including context, as a way to increase transparency and help shareholders hold boards to account about executive pay (Department for Business, Energy and Industrial Strategy 2017).

---

1 Or indeed changes of business practice driven by twitterstorms of activist disapproval, as distinct from genuine shifts in consumer opinion.

Consequently, the Companies (Miscellaneous Reporting) Regulations 2018 now require UK quoted companies with more than 250 UK employees to disclose pay ratio information and to account for the results and for any changes over time.

The figures must be set out in a table within the annual directors' remuneration report. The figures that should be reported are the CEO's total pay as a ratio to the median, the 25th percentile and the 75th percentile. Eventually, the table must include these ratios for the previous ten years.

Beneath the table of figures, companies must provide supporting information and explanation including the methodology chosen for calculating the ratios and the reason for any changes in the ratios from the previous year. For the median ratio (50th percentile), the company must explain whether the company believes that this indicator is consistent with the company's general employee pay, reward and progression policies and, if so, why. The information, like the requirements for reporting on gender and ethnic pay gaps, will be costly and irksome for companies to provide in the required format.

In addition, a 'naming and shaming' register is being set up listing any FTSE all-share company where at least one in five shareholders have voted against company pay policy in the last year.

It is unclear quite why this information will be of more than passing interest to shareholders. Few are likely to be influenced, in deciding whether to vote for or against incumbent management, by pay structures – any more than they would be by a description and explanation of the capital equipment used or the real estate occupied by the company.

Most FTSE-100 company shares are held by overseas investors who may be much less concerned about pay issues than the British. The ultimate beneficiaries of UK shares are very often passive investors via pension funds or other financial intermediaries. These intermediaries are usually required to serve their clients' interests by securing the highest possible return on their investments without getting involved in questions about appropriate levels of pay or double-guessing the management. If they are unhappy with the stewardship of the company, they can sell their shares.

But if the bulk of shareholders may not be concerned, the media and political activists will no doubt pick up on what they see as particularly noxious pay ratios. From what we have seen with gender pay gap figures, few will note any nuances.

Thus CEOs in the retail sector, where average pay is low, will probably be castigated for their high ratios, while CEOs on similar pay in the financial sector, where average pay is higher, may escape censure.

Company managements are likely to react to this arbitrary threat of unfavourable publicity (and demands for action) in a number of ways. They may indeed reduce or moderate the growth of the headline pay of CEOs and other top management, as the government intends. But they might also take evasive action. For example, they may escape scrutiny by reducing the headcount of employees.

This could be done by outsourcing workers,[2] particularly those on low pay. This could well be disadvantageous to these employees, casualties in somebody else's campaign against high pay.

One possible unanticipated consequence might be firms reducing or eliminating the performance-related part of CEO pay, as otherwise a successful run of results could boost the recorded pay ratio and put the company under an unwanted spotlight. As a frequent complaint is that top pay is insufficiently sensitive to results, this would be a perverse outcome.[3]

In the longer term, companies may choose to delist and go private, or else switch company headquarters to another jurisdiction, to avoid this scrutiny. Given that three-quarters of the revenue of FTSE-100 companies is earned outside the UK,[4] this may make sense. And certainly some newer companies considering issuing shares in this country might pause before doing so.

Another possibility is that, while top pay may be reduced or held down, firms will compensate their senior

---

2 UK employees are defined as those employed under a contract of service, except people employed to work wholly or mainly outside the UK. Contractors or agency workers are not included because they are employed under a contract with a different organisation. Individual contractors and consultants with a personal contract with the company but who may contract for services to other companies would typically not be included in the headcount either.

3 I owe this point to Ryan Bourne.

4 Tracker funds – three questions to ask before investing, Hargreaves Lansdown, 11 September 2017 (https://www.hl.co.uk/news/articles/archive/tracker-funds-three-questions-to-ask-before-investing).

management in other ways. For example, as occurred in the past when incomes policies held pay down and very high marginal tax rates anyway made large nominal salaries less attractive, we may see an expansion of the 'perks' associated with senior management – company cars, jets, luxurious offices and so forth. This proliferation of company expense was a significant concern in the 1960s, as mentioned in Chapter 3, and led future Nobel Prize winner Oliver Williamson (1964) to develop an influential theoretical model with a managerial utility function incorporating staff expense.

A further implication might be that another aspect of the reward structure is affected: namely the risk of losing jobs. UK chief executives may be highly paid, but the corollary is that both in the private[5] and the public (see, for example, Timmins 2016) sectors the likelihood of being dismissed for poor performance has increased. This is, in a sense, part of the deal. But if rewards for these risky posts are reduced, it is likely that potential applicants will seek guarantees of greater job security when taking a post. This may affect both the quality of applicants and the behaviour of boards, not necessarily for the better.

Workers on the board

One frequently touted policy is a requirement for large firms to have employee representatives on boards and/or

---

5   UK CEOs have less time than ever to make their mark, PwC, 15 May 2017 (https://www.pwc.co.uk/press-room/press-releases/uk-ceos-have-less -time-than-ever-to-make-an-impact.html).

remuneration committees. These representatives would, it is argued, exercise a restraining influence on pay deals for top executives. This seems to be a policy with considerable support among employees.[6]

Theresa May appeared to promise that she would impose employee representation on boards during her campaign to become Prime Minister. She subsequently backed away from this position as a result of pressure from cabinet colleagues and business organisations.[7]

The Labour Party, however, now seems to have made a binding commitment to such a policy, although its proposals are not just focused on high executive pay but are aimed at a wider reorientation of company policies to break from what Jeremy Corbyn has called a 'reckless corporate culture' which has in his view exploited workers and damaged Britain's economy. Another aspect of this is John McDonnell's plan to require firms to give workers shares in their businesses.[8]

At Labour's Annual Conference in Liverpool in September 2018, Mr Corbyn outlined plans which would require companies (public or private) with a workforce of 250 or more to reserve at least a third of positions in the

---

6   Public support employee representatives on boards, Survation (https://www.survation.com/public-support-employee-representatives-on-boards/).

7   John Lewis and CBI object to plans for employees on boards, *Drapers*, 3 November 2016 (https://www.drapersonline.com/retail/john-lewis-and-cbi-object-to-plans-for-employees-on-boards/7013553.article).

8   Labour conference: John McDonnell unveils shares plan for workers, BBC News, 24 September 2018 (https://www.bbc.co.uk/news/uk-politics-45621361).

boardroom for employee representatives. These employee directors would be elected by the workforce and paid at a level equal to other board members.[9]

We cannot predict how these precise proposals would be implemented and how they would affect pay. However, the experience elsewhere of employee representation on boards does not suggest that board representation in itself has much impact. Germany and France have such representation, but both countries (Germany in particular) have some very highly paid executives. In 2017 the highest-paid CEO of a German company, for instance, earned €21.8 million.[10]

If German experience is anything to go by, though, employee representatives will largely be union activists. They are unlikely to confine their concerns to executive pay, or even the pay of the workforce as a whole, but will also want to influence wider issues such as investment policy, mergers and plant expansion or closure. Indeed, this is what the Labour Party wants to see as it promotes 'democracy in the workplace'.

German unions have traditionally been more moderate than those in the UK, but even in Germany unions have acted as an inhibiting force on large companies where

---

9   Workers to make up one third of company board members under Labour, Jeremy Corbyn vows, *The Independent*, 23 September 2018 (https://www.in dependent.co.uk/news/uk/politics/jeremy-corbyn-workers-boards-la bour-conference-one-third-union-a8550946.html).

10 German executive pay gets supersized, *Handelsblatt*, 15 March 2018 (https://global.handelsblatt.com/companies/german-executive-pay-gets -supersized-898574).

there is codetermination.[11] Gorton and Schmid (2000), in a much-quoted study, claim that employee resistance to restructuring cost West German firms about 26 per cent of shareholder value in the period after reunification. There is no reason to suppose that employee representation on UK boards would be any less likely to inhibit necessary change: rather more likely, if anything, given the historical record of UK unions. So adding compulsory worker representation on boards might well slow productivity growth in larger firms.

Binding pay ratios and upper limits on pay

Unease about high pay in the public sector led the coalition government to set up an enquiry under Will Hutton, a long-standing critic of high pay. It was expected to lead to a cap on the ratio of chief executive to lowest-paid worker, rumoured to be 20 to 1. However, Hutton's report (2011) rejected such a cap. He reflected that the extent of high pay in the public sector was exaggerated and that a hard-and-fast rule would be difficult to maintain given the way ratios can be manipulated. More fundamentally, he pointed out that 'the UK must take care to avoid making the public sector a fundamentally unattractive place for those with talent and drive' (Hutton 2011: 10).

Nevertheless, there are now substantial restrictions on top public sector salaries. Any new salary above £150,000

---

11 The *Mitbestimmung* laws mandate employee representation of just under half of the supervisory board in firms with more than 2,000 employees: for companies with 500–1,999 employees a third are elected.

in the public sector has to be signed off by the Cabinet Office. This restriction has been extended to institutions which are not, strictly speaking, in the public sector. For instance the pay of university vice-chancellors and other senior university staff is now regulated by the Office for Students, and any salary over £150,000 has in effect to be approved by one man, Sir Michael Barber, an ex-Labour Party political activist who has threatened universities with large fines if they don't convince him of their arguments for higher pay packages.[12]

The £150,000 figure is arbitrary, but seems to have originated in a rough assessment of the Prime Minister's salary. However, it is unclear why this is a reasonable basis for setting pay limits. Apart from the prestige associated with the role, prime ministers have accommodation and a whole range of services provided for them. Moreover, their salary has been repeatedly held down for political purposes. Some prime ministers have had private incomes or high-earning spouses. In any case, they can expect vastly higher incomes in retirement from memoirs, speaking engagements, prestige international roles and so forth.

The value of this £150,000 limit will shrink year on year in real terms with inflation and tax increases. At some stage the limit will have to be raised, but what government will dare to raise it? Fixed upper limits are worse than pay ratios in this respect.

---

12 Universities could face 'significant' fines over vice-chancellor pay packages, regulator warns, *The Independent*, 19 June 2018 (https://www.independent .co.uk/news/education/education-news/vice-chancellor-pay-universities -fines-office-for-students-regulator-michael-barber-a8403506.html).

If the current government is trying to hold down public and quasi-public sector salaries, the Labour Party wishes to restrict pay for a wider group of high earners. It now intends to impose a 20 to 1 ratio beyond the current public sector – on the utilities which it intends to renationalise,[13] and even on businesses which bid for public sector work. Jeremy Corbyn says that his government would

> extend that to any company that is awarded a govern-ment contract. A 20:1 ratio means someone earning the living wage, just over £16,000 a year, would permit an ex-ecutive to be earning nearly £350,000. It cannot be right that if companies are getting public money that can be creamed off by a few at the top.[14]

It remains to be seen how exactly this would work. Mr Corbyn clearly has in mind such *bêtes noires* as Capita and G4S, whose business largely consists of work for the gov-ernment and whose sometimes poor performance has not prevented their CEOs from receiving pay packages worth many millions.

Government outsourcing is a market worth well over £100 billion annually,[15] and involves a huge range of com-

---

13 John McDonnell targets water bosses in renationalisation plan, *The Guard-ian*, 24 September 2018 (https://www.theguardian.com/politics/2018/sep/24/john-mcdonnell-targets-water-bosses-in-renationalisation-plan).

14 Corbyn calls for wage cap on bosses at government contractors, *The Guard-ian*, 10 January 2017 (https://www.theguardian.com/politics/2017/jan/10/corbyn-proposes-maximum-wage-for-all-government-contractors).

15 Services contracted out to the private sector include everything from accounting services to advertising to pest control. For many of these

panies for whom government work, however, may be a minor source of revenue. To this might be added many billions of pounds of government procurement – everything from nuclear submarines to office furniture, from hospital beds to paperclips. If Labour is serious about this, presumably the same restrictions should be placed on companies providing goods as on those providing services.

If so, firms which were not heavily committed to providing goods and services to the public sector would avoid this kind of provision rather than have their pay structures dictated by, and presumably intrusively monitored by, a government regulator.

The result would be that competition for government procurement would be reduced. Prices would therefore tend to rise, and in some cases government might find that no private providers would be forthcoming at all, perhaps forcing the government to take services in-house at higher cost and to buy goods from overseas suppliers.

Squeezed pay distributions

A little-discussed implication of restrictions on top pay is the consequences for pay structures within organisations. One train of reasoning in the economic analysis of pay is provided by tournament theory (Lazear and Rosen 1981).

The argument here is that high executive pay acts as a motivator for other people within an organisation. A high

---

contractors the government may only account for a small part of their business. A partial listing is provided at: http://www.crsvat.com/wp-content/uploads/2015/06/CRS_A4-COS-List_v4.pdf

salary for top executives relative to other staff motivates people at the next level down to work harder to secure eventual promotion. Thus restricting top rewards might have adverse effects on the effort of employees lower down organisations.

Supporters of this approach point to the evidence of sporting tournaments. A classic study of the European professional golf tour (Ehrenberg and Bognanno 1990) has often been cited: these authors claimed that those tour events with a bigger gap between the reward for the winner and for the runners-up elicited greater effort from the participants. This was indicated by lower average scores (controlling for weather and other special factors) from the contestants.

Frick (2003) has argued that the evidence from a wider range of sporting tournaments is less conclusive, and in any case it would be difficult to argue that the scale of rewards for top CEOs is always indicative of an optimal pay structure. Nevertheless, tournament theory does direct attention to pay structures rather than simply top pay.

And certainly tight pay caps imposed in some areas might have negative effects. For example, holding down university vice-chancellors' pay year after year would necessarily also hold down the next levels of pay for pro-vice-chancellors, deans and other managers. As senior academics such as professors can earn substantial amounts from their basic pay and outside consultancies, it could become increasingly difficult to attract academics to take on institutional leadership roles.

The same arguments apply within the civil service and local government, where specialists such as scientists, computer experts, accountants, lawyers and economists have potential earnings in the private sector which considerably exceed those in the public sector. They are also applicable in those industries which the Labour Party seeks to renationalise. Over time, fewer specialists are likely to find it attractive to move into top roles, leaving the field to generalists with little depth of knowledge and competence in many areas of the organisations they run.

International competition

It would certainly be difficult to attract good overseas applicants for vice-chancellor roles, when similar posts in other English-speaking countries already pay much more generously. Two years ago eight US college presidents were earning over $2 million (£1.5 million). Nine Australian vice-chancellors earned more than A$1 million (£600,000). In Canada, as far back as 2010, Ontario's top university boss was being paid more than C$1 million (£600,000). Even in New Zealand, the University of Auckland's vice-chancellor earns more than NZ$710,000 (£400,000).[16]

More generally, the UK operates in an international market for executive talent and needs the freedom to pay internationally competitive salaries. This assertion is often dismissed by pointing to the relatively few UK nationals who operate in top jobs abroad. However, this is not the point at all. The international market works both ways,

---

16 UK vice-chancellors are not overpaid, *Times Higher Education*, 3 August 2017 (https://www.timeshighereducation.com/opinion/uk-vice-chancellors-are-not-overpaid).

and the UK has benefited from inflows of top business talent in the same way that the Premier League has gained from an influx of foreign footballing talent – despite few English footballers ever playing abroad.

In 2017, 40 per cent of FTSE-100 companies were headed by non-UK nationals, from twenty different countries;[17] 30 per cent of Board Chairs and Chief Financial Officers were also born abroad. No other leading exchange had more than a third of its CEOs drawn from non-nationals. The US and France had less than 10 per cent. No other country, incidentally, has as the head of its central bank a non-national: few allow non-nationals to occupy senior civil service positions.

The UK, then, has one of the most internationally diverse and open business leaderships in the world, something we need to maintain and build on after Brexit. The danger with tighter regulation of top pay is that some of the highly skilled UK nationals who are mobile will move abroad and we lose the prospect of similarly skilled people coming into the country. The result of a shortage of talent in relation to the demand for it would probably be lost output.

Longer term

The current political focus is on pay for corporate executives, heads of public sector organisations, universities and charities. This is already a very large number of organisations for

---

17 Number of foreign-born CEOs in the UK doubles, *Economia*, 13 March 2017 (https://economia.icaew.com/news/march-2017/number-of-foreign-born -ceos-in-the-uk-doubles).

a range of regulators to monitor. When added to existing controls on public sector pay and the ever-increasing scope of minimum wages, further expansion of government's influence over pay will soon be reaching levels last seen in the days of the Prices and Income Commission.

Yet these interventions have grown up in an ad hoc manner and are likely to produce inconsistent results, which will lead to pressure for greater control and greater uniformity in pay, which would shift the labour market further away from market forces and closer to a pay structure determined by politicians and effectively unaccountable regulators. There is no reason to suppose that they would be particularly good at this task.

Moreover, why stop at listed company executives? Currently, there is little pressure to regulate the pay of such individual high-earners as entrepreneurs, people in private equity, top sportsmen and women, fashion models and movie stars. Yet we have already seen a backlash against the high pay of BBC TV presenters, with social media anger leading managers to pressure people such as John Humphrys to accept 'voluntary' cuts in pay. Some have moved out to private radio stations to avoid this sort of pressure. But this bolt-hole may not be open indefinitely.

Claims are made that chief executives of quoted companies are in a 'rigged' market which exaggerates their contribution to their organisations; that government has a right to insist that public servants (whether in the civil service, local authorities, future nationalised industries or the BBC) should have their pay limited; and that vice-chancellors or charity heads, though not directly employed by the state, nevertheless receive income and privileges from government and thus should be 'accountable' to it. Other people who come outside these categories might be threatened if their activities were felt to be reprehensible in some way.

Once the principle is established of interfering with private sector businesses through restrictions on their ability to pay whatever salaries they wish, or by imposing worker representation, the barrier to further incursions into property rights is lowered. Calls are being made for large private businesses to be subject to similar disclosure rules as listed companies. Denise Coates, the founder of Bet365, the online betting company, has no obligations to outside shareholders. But she has attracted hostility from activists for the large amounts she has paid herself from profits which accrue in part from gambling addiction.[18] Large numbers of entrepreneurs might fall foul of some group or other if fairness is to be judged on the basis of a beauty contest.

It is in any case doubtful that antipathy towards high pay will continue to be confined to large businesses. It is more likely that it will increasingly be considered 'unfair' that there should be huge disparities of income, whatever their origin. In an environment where some of these 'inequities' have been reduced or removed, there is a clear possibility that there will be demands for reducing the pay of other people who fall into the category of 'the 1 per cent' – either through further regulation or much higher levels of personal income tax.

---

18 Bet365 chief Denise Coates paid herself £217m last year, *The Guardian*, 12 November 2017 (https://www.theguardian.com/business/2017/nov/12/bet365-chief-denise-coates-paid-217m-last-year).

This would be worrying on grounds of personal liberty. But it would also have implications for the ordinary taxpayer.

At present around 28 per cent of income tax is paid by the top 1 per cent of earners, up from 21 per cent in 1999.[19] Over the same period the share of income tax paid by the bottom 50 per cent of earners has fallen from 12.6 per cent to under 10 per cent. Some individuals pay enormous amounts of tax. For instance, during the last election campaign Lord Sugar posted on social media an image of a cheque he had recently paid HMRC: it was for £58 million.[20]

If top pay is forced down, some highly paid individuals will move abroad, and pay no UK taxes. Those who remain would be earning less, and would pay lower taxes. Assuming public spending remains the same (or more likely increases, whichever government is in power), the logical conclusion is that taxes would have to increase for middle and lower earners.

Conclusion

It is understandable that the public dislikes huge discrepancies in earnings, and may well feel that much high pay is

---

19 Do the top 1% of earners pay 28% of the tax burden? Full Fact (https://fullfact.org/economy/do-top-1-earners-pay-28-tax-burden/).

20 Election 2017: Lord Sugar reveals £58m tax payment after row with Jeremy Corbyn supporters. *The Independent*, 8 June 2017 (https://www.independent.co.uk/News/business/news/election-2017-alan-sugar-tax-payment-58-million-jeremy-corbyn-supporters-labour-peer-lord-hmrc-a7778831.html).

undeserved, or even corruptly obtained. But reducing top earnings would have no discernible positive effect on the income of people at the bottom of the pay distribution. It could well, directly or indirectly, negatively affect the pre- and post-tax incomes of middle earners.

Governments need to be careful in how they react to populist calls for action. The current requirement for leading plcs to spell out the basis of their pay structure, while it could lead to adverse consequences, may be acceptable. But giving government the power to fix pay ratios or even pay caps brings dangers which are not sufficiently discussed by those demanding action.

Moving to a world where the state – influenced by constant pressure from activists on social media – fixes pay for top earners, and indirectly therefore for employees all the way down the pay hierarchy, would be a radical step. It would be a world very different from that we have known in peacetime. It would make all pay increases highly politicised, as was the case with incomes policies in the 1960s and 1970s, and strain the competence of government, already stretched much too far. It would surely lead eventually to lower growth and productivity.

While some on the left might deny this, and in any case place equality for its own sake high on their agenda, it is disappointing to see so many of those ostensibly favouring free markets and limited government join the clamour against high pay.

REFERENCES

Bertrand, M., Black, S. E., Jensen, S. and Lleras-Muney, A. (2019) Breaking the glass ceiling? The effect of board quotas on female labour market outcomes in Norway. *Review of Economic Studies* 86(1): 191–239.

Bikhchandani, S., Hirshleifer, D. and Welch, I. (1992) A theory of fads, fashion, custom, and cultural change as informational cascades. *Journal of Political Economy* 100(5): 992–1026.

Black, F. and Scholes, M. (1973) The pricing of options and corporate liabilities. *Journal of Political Economy* 81(3): 637–54.

Bonestroo, J. (2017) CEO incentive-based compensation, investment opportunities and institutional heterogeneity. University of Groningen and Uppsala University.

Bourne, R. and Shackleton, J. R. (2017) Getting the state out of pre-school and childcare. Discussion Paper 81. London: Institute of Economic Affairs.

Brynjolfsson, E. and McAfee, A. (2011) *Race Against the Machine: How the Digital Revolution is Accelerating Innovation, Driving Productivity, and Irreversibly Transforming Employment and the Economy.* Lexington, MA: Digital Frontier Press.

CFA Society UK (2017) *An Analysis of CEO Pay Arrangements and Value Creation for FTSE-350 Companies.* London: CFA Society of the UK.

Committee of University Chairs (2014) *The Higher Education Code of Governance.* Bristol: CUC.

Committee of University Chairs (2015) *Governing Body and Remuneration Committee Practice on Senior Staff Remuneration*. Bristol: CUC.

Committee of University Chairs (2018) *The Higher Education Senior Staff Remuneration Code*. Bristol: CUC.

Correa, R. and Lel, U. (2016) Say on pay laws, executive compensation, pay slice, and firm valuation around the world. *Journal of Financial Economics* 122(3): 500–20.

Costa Dias, M., Joyce, R. and Parodi, F. (2018) The gender pay gap in the UK: children and experience in work. Institute for Fiscal Studies Working Paper 18/02.

Crawford, C., Crawford, R. and Jin, W. (2014) Estimating the public cost of student loans. London: Institute for Fiscal Studies.

Department for Business, Energy and Industrial Strategy (2016) Corporate Governance Reform Green Paper. London: BEIS.

Department for Business, Energy and Industrial Strategy (2017) Corporate Governance Reform: The Government Response to the Green Paper Consultation. London: BEIS.

Dustmann, C., Fitzenberger, B., Schönberg, U. and Spitz-Oener, A. (2014) From sick man of Europe to economic superstar: Germany's resurgent economy. *Journal of Economic Perspectives* 28(1): 167–88.

Edmans, A. (2011) Does the stock market fully value intangibles? Employee satisfaction and equity prices. *Journal of Financial Economics* 101(3): 621–40.

Edmans, A. (2012) The link between job satisfaction and firm value, with implications for corporate social responsibility. *Academy of Management Perspectives* 26(4): 1–19.

Edmans, A., Gabaix, X. and Jenter, D. (2017) Executive compensation: a survey of theory and evidence. In *The Handbook of the Economics of Corporate Governance* (ed. B. Hermalin and M. Weisback). Amsterdam: North Holland.

Ehrenberg, R. G. and Bognanno, M. L. (1990) Do tournaments have incentive effects? *Journal of Political Economy* 98(6): 1307–24.

Epstein, R. (1992) *Forbidden Grounds: The Case Against Employment Discrimination Laws*. Cambridge, MA: Harvard University Press.

Equality Trust (2017) *Pay Tracker: Comparing Chief Executive Officer Pay in the FTSE 100 with Average Pay and Low Pay in the UK*. London: The Equality Trust.

Faleye, O., Reis, E. and Venkateswaran, A. (2013) The determinants and effects of CEO–employee pay ratios. *Journal of Banking and Finance* 37(8): 3258–72.

Financial Conduct Authority (2016) *Interim Report of the Asset Management Market Study*. London: Financial Conduct Authority.

Financial Reporting Council (2018) *The Wates Corporate Governance Principles for Large Private Companies*. London: Financial Reporting Council.

Flammer, C. and Bansal, P. (2016) Does a long-term orientation create value? Evidence from a regression discontinuity. Available at SSRN: https://ssrn.com/abstract=2511507

Frick, B. (2003) Contest theory and sport. *Oxford Review of Economic Policy* 19(4): 512–30.

Frydman, C. and Saks, R. (2010) Executive compensation: a new view from a long-term perspective, 1936–2005. *Review of Financial Studies* 23(5): 2099–138.

Gabaix, X. and Landier, A. (2008) Why has CEO pay increased so much? *Quarterly Journal of Economics* 123(1): 49–100.

Goldin, C. (2015) How to achieve gender equality. *Milken Institute Review*, Third Quarter: 24–33.

Goldin, C. and Katz, L. (2008) *The Race Between Technology and Education*. Cambridge, MA: Harvard.

Gorton, G. and Schmid, F. (2000) Class struggle inside the firm: a study of German codetermination. National Bureau for Economic Research Working Paper 7945.

Hayek, F. A. (1976) The atavism of social justice. In *New Studies in Philosophy, Politics, Economics and the History of Ideas.* London: Routledge and Kegan Paul.

Hicks, J. (1963) [1932] *The Theory of Wages*, 2nd edn. London: Palgrave Macmillan.

High Pay Centre (2013) *Global CEO Appointments: A Very Domestic Issue*. London: High Pay Centre.

High Pay Centre (2015a) *Made to Measure: How Opinion about Executive Performance Becomes Fact*. London: High Pay Centre.

High Pay Centre (2015b) *No Routine Riches: Reforms to Performance-Related Pay*. London: High Pay Centre.

High Pay Centre (2015c) *Pay Ratios? Just Do It*. London: High Pay Centre.

High Pay Centre and Chartered Institute of Personnel and Development (2018) *Executive Pay: Review of FTSE-100 Executive Pay*. London: CIPD.

House of Commons (2017) Business, Energy and Industrial Strategy Committee, Corporate Governance Fourth Report of Session 2016-7 HC 702.

Hutton Review of Fair Pay in the Public Sector (2011) *Final Report*. London: HM Treasury.

Institute for Fiscal Studies (2018) *2018 Annual Report on Education Spending in England*. London: Institute for Fiscal Studies.

International Finance Corporation (2015) *A Guide to Corporate Governance Practices in the European Union*. Washington, DC: World Bank.

International Labor Organization (2015) *Women in Business and Management: Gaining Momentum*. Geneva: ILO.

Investment Association (2016) *Executive Remuneration Working Group Final Report*. London: Investment Association.

Investment Association (2017) *Clients and Asset Allocation*. London: Investment Association.

Jensen, M. C. and Murphy, K. J. (1990) Performance pay and top-management incentives. *Journal of Political Economy* 98(2): 225–64.

Kampkötter, P. (2015) Non-executive compensation in German and Swiss banks before and after the financial crisis. *European Journal of Finance* 21(15): 1297–316.

Kaplan, S. N. and Rauh, J. (2013) It's the market: the broad-based rise in the return to top talent. *Journal of Economic Perspectives* 27(3): 35–56.

Kay Review of Equity Markets and Long-Term Decision-Making (2012) *Interim Report*. London: Department for Business, Innovation and Skills.

Lazear, E. and Rosen, S. (1981) Rank order tournaments as optimum labour contracts. *Journal of Political Economy* 89(5): 841–64.

Lucas, J. R. (2013) What should we be paid? *The Oxford Magazine*, Noughth Week, Trinity Term.

Manifest/MM&K (2012) Executive Director Total Remuneration Survey.

Mankiw, N. G. (2013) Defending the one percent. *Journal of Economic Perspectives* 27(3): 21–34.

Marchionatti, R. (2004) *Early Mathematical Economics 1871–1915: Volume 2*. London: Routledge.

Marshall, A. (1890) *Principles of Economics*. London: Macmillan.

Mueller, H. M., Ouimet, P. O. and Simintzi, E. (2017) Within-firm Pay Inequality. *Review of Financial Studies* 30(10): 3605–35.

NEST Corporation (2017) *Looking after Members' Money: NEST's Investment Approach*. London: NEST Corporation.

Norge Bank (2017) *Remuneration of the CEO: Asset Manager Perspective*. Oslo: Norge Bank Investment Management.

Norton, W. (2014) *Transparency Begins at Home: Why Charities Must State Who Funds Them*. London: Centre for Policy Studies.

Office for National Statistics (2017) Annual Survey of Hours and Earnings, 2017 provisional results and 2016 revised results.

Oxford Economics (2017) *The Economic Impact of Universities in 2014–15: Report for Universities UK*. Oxford: Oxford Economics.

Piketty, T. and Saez, E. (2006) The evolution of top incomes: a historical and international perspective. *American Economic Review* 96(2): 200–205.

Purposeful Company (2017) *Executive Remuneration Report*. London: Big Innovation Centre.

Record, N. (2014) *The £600 Billion Question: How Public Sector Pension Liabilities Are Being Undervalued at the Expense of Future Generations*. London: Intergenerational Foundation.

Rosen, S. (1981) The economics of superstars. *American Economic Review* 71(5): 845–58.

Rouen, E. (2017) Rethinking measurement of pay disparity and its relation to firm performance. Harvard Business School Working Paper 18-007.

Schelling, T. C. (1973) Hockey helmets, concealed weapons, and daylight saving: a study of binary choices with externalities. *Journal of Conflict Resolution* 17(3): 381–428.

Schumpeter, J. A. (1934) *The Theory of Economic Development.* Oxford University Press

Simon, H. A. (1955) A behavioral model of rational choice. *The Quarterly Journal of Economics*, 69(1): 99–118.

Timmins, N. (2016) *The Chief Executive's Tale: Views from the Front Line of the NHS.* London: King's Fund.

Trades Union Congress (2015) *A Culture of Excess: The Pay of FTSE 100 Remuneration Committee Members.* London: TUC.

Von Lilienfeld-Toal, U. and Ruenzi, S. (2014) CEO ownership, stock market performance, and managerial discretion. *Journal of Finance* 69(3): 1013–50.

Watts, D. J. (2002) A simple model of global cascades on random networks. *Proceedings of the National Academy of Sciences* 99(9): 5766–71.

Williamson, O. E. (1964) *The Economics of Discretionary Behaviour.* New York: Prentice-Hall.

Wilkinson, R. and Pickett, K. (2009) *The Spirit Level: Why Greater Equality Makes Societies Stronger.* London: Allen Lane.

ABOUT THE IEA

The Institute is a research and educational charity (No. CC 235 351), limited by guarantee. Its mission is to improve understanding of the fundamental institutions of a free society by analysing and expounding the role of markets in solving economic and social problems.

The IEA achieves its mission by:

- a high-quality publishing programme
- conferences, seminars, lectures and other events
- outreach to school and college students
- brokering media introductions and appearances

The IEA, which was established in 1955 by the late Sir Antony Fisher, is an educational charity, not a political organisation. It is independent of any political party or group and does not carry on activities intended to affect support for any political party or candidate in any election or referendum, or at any other time. It is financed by sales of publications, conference fees and voluntary donations.

In addition to its main series of publications, the IEA also publishes (jointly with the University of Buckingham), *Economic Affairs*.

The IEA is aided in its work by a distinguished international Academic Advisory Council and an eminent panel of Honorary Fellows. Together with other academics, they review prospective IEA publications, their comments being passed on anonymously to authors. All IEA papers are therefore subject to the same rigorous independent refereeing process as used by leading academic journals.

IEA publications enjoy widespread classroom use and course adoptions in schools and universities. They are also sold throughout the world and often translated/reprinted.

Since 1974 the IEA has helped to create a worldwide network of 100 similar institutions in over 70 countries. They are all independent but share the IEA's mission.

Views expressed in the IEA's publications are those of the authors, not those of the Institute (which has no corporate view), its Managing Trustees, Academic Advisory Council members or senior staff.

Members of the Institute's Academic Advisory Council, Honorary Fellows, Trustees and Staff are listed on the following page.

The Institute gratefully acknowledges financial support for its publications programme and other work from a generous benefaction by the late Professor Ronald Coase.

Other books recently published by the IEA include:

Classical Liberalism – A Primer
Eamonn Butler
Readings in Political Economy 2; ISBN 978-0-255-36707-3; £10.00

Federal Britain: The Case for Decentralisation
Philip Booth
Readings in Political Economy 3; ISBN 978-0-255-36713-4; £10.00

Forever Contemporary: The Economics of Ronald Coase
Edited by Cento Veljanovski
Readings in Political Economy 4; ISBN 978-0-255-36710-3; £15.00

Power Cut? How the EU Is Pulling the Plug on Electricity Markets
Carlo Stagnaro
Hobart Paperback 180; ISBN 978-0-255-36716-5; £10.00

Policy Stability and Economic Growth – Lessons from the Great Recession
John B. Taylor
Readings in Political Economy 5; ISBN 978-0-255-36719-6; £7.50

Breaking Up Is Hard To Do: Britain and Europe's Dysfunctional Relationship
Edited by Patrick Minford and J. R. Shackleton
Hobart Paperback 181; ISBN 978-0-255-36722-6; £15.00

In Focus: The Case for Privatising the BBC
Edited by Philip Booth
Hobart Paperback 182; ISBN 978-0-255-36725-7; £12.50

Islamic Foundations of a Free Society
Edited by Nouh El Harmouzi and Linda Whetstone
Hobart Paperback 183; ISBN 978-0-255-36728-8; £12.50

The Economics of International Development: Foreign Aid versus Freedom for the World's Poor
William Easterly
Readings in Political Economy 6; ISBN 978-0-255-36731-8; £7.50

Taxation, Government Spending and Economic Growth
Edited by Philip Booth
Hobart Paperback 184; ISBN 978-0-255-36734-9; £15.00

Universal Healthcare without the NHS: Towards a Patient-Centred Health System
Kristian Niemietz
Hobart Paperback 185; ISBN 978-0-255-36737-0; £10.00

Sea Change: How Markets and Property Rights Could Transform the Fishing Industry
Edited by Richard Wellings
Readings in Political Economy 7; ISBN 978-0-255-36740-0; £10.00

Working to Rule: The Damaging Economics of UK Employment Regulation
J. R. Shackleton
Hobart Paperback 186; ISBN 978-0-255-36743-1; £15.00

Education, War and Peace: The Surprising Success of Private Schools in War-Torn Countries
James Tooley and David Longfield
ISBN 978-0-255-36746-2; £10.00

Killjoys: A Critique of Paternalism
Christopher Snowdon
ISBN 978-0-255-36749-3; £12.50

Financial Stability without Central Banks
George Selgin, Kevin Dowd and Mathieu Bédard
ISBN 978-0-255-36752-3; £10.00

Against the Grain: Insights from an Economic Contrarian
Paul Ormerod
ISBN 978-0-255-36755-4; £15.00

Ayn Rand: An Introduction
Eamonn Butler
ISBN 978-0-255-36764-6; £12.50

Capitalism: An Introduction
Eamonn Butler
ISBN 978-0-255-36758-5; £12.50

Opting Out: Conscience and Cooperation in a Pluralistic Society
David S. Oderberg
ISBN 978-0-255-36761-5; £12.50

Getting the Measure of Money: A Critical Assessment of UK Monetary Indicators
Anthony J. Evans
ISBN 978-0-255-36767-7; £12.50

Socialism: The Failed Idea That Never Dies
Kristian Niemietz
ISBN 978-0-255-36770-7; £17.50

Other IEA publications

Comprehensive information on other publications and the wider work of the IEA can be found at www.iea.org.uk. To order any publication please see below.

Personal customers

Orders from personal customers should be directed to the IEA:

Clare Rusbridge
IEA
2 Lord North Street
FREEPOST LON10168
London SW1P 3YZ
Tel: 020 7799 8907. Fax: 020 7799 2137
Email: sales@iea.org.uk

Trade customers

All orders from the book trade should be directed to the IEA's distributor:

NBN International (IEA Orders)
Orders Dept.
NBN International
10 Thornbury Road
Plymouth PL6 7PP
Tel: 01752 202301, Fax: 01752 202333
Email: orders@nbninternational.com

IEA subscriptions

The IEA also offers a subscription service to its publications. For a single annual payment (currently £42.00 in the UK), subscribers receive every monograph the IEA publishes. For more information please contact:

Clare Rusbridge
Subscriptions
IEA
2 Lord North Street
FREEPOST LON10168
London SW1P 3YZ
Tel: 020 7799 8907, Fax: 020 7799 2137
Email: crusbridge@iea.org.uk